D0171780

# Fairy Tales, Fables, Legends, and Myths
## USING FOLK LITERATURE IN YOUR CLASSROOM

**FRONTISPIECE**   A Navajo Indian boy enjoys an Italian folk tale.

# Fairy Tales, Fables, Legends, and Myths

## USING FOLK LITERATURE IN YOUR CLASSROOM

Second Edition

## Bette Bosma

TEACHERS COLLEGE, COLUMBIA UNIVERSITY
NEW YORK AND LONDON

Published by Teachers College Press, 1234 Amsterdam Avenue
New York, NY 10027

*Library of Congress Cataloging-in-Publication Data*

Bosma, Bette, 1927–
    Fairy tales, fables, legends, and myths : using folk literature in your classroom / Bette Bosma.—2nd ed.
        p.    cm.
    Includes bibliographical references (p.    ) and index.
    ISBN 0-8077-3134-X
    1. Folklore and education—United States.    2. Folk literature—Study and teaching (Elementary)—United States.    3. Reading (Elementary)—United States.    4. English language—United States—Composition and exercises.    5. Activity programs in education—United States.    I. Title.
    LB1583.8.B67    1992                                                        92-3915

Printed on acid-free paper

Manufactured in the United States of America

99 98 97 96 95 94 93 92    8 7 6 5 4 3 2 1

# Contents

Preface                                                                vii

1. The Tale                                                              1
   The Importance of Folk Literature for Children                        1
   Adapting Folktales                                                    6
   Folklore Classifications and Definitions                              8
   Preview                                                              13

2. Folk Literature in Multicultural Education                           15
   The Many Cultures in America                                         15
   Translation of Folk Literature                                       19
   Book Illustration and Cultural Understanding                         20
   International Studies                                                 22
   Summary                                                              24

3. Understanding the Story                                              26
   Reading Aloud                                                        26
   Guiding Reading Comprehension                                        30
   Vocabulary Development                                               37
   Summary                                                              42

4. Critical Reading                                                     43
   Classifying Types and Characteristics                                44
   Making Relevant Comparisons                                          47
   Making Judgments                                                     54
   Recognizing Themes                                                   58
   Summary                                                              61

5. Learning to Write with Folk Literature                               63
   Folktale Form                                                        64

Folktale Theme and Content                                    70
Summary                                                       82

6.  *Creative Activities with Folk Literature*                84
    Improvising, Pantomiming, Dramatizing                     84
    Mask Making                                               86
    Storytelling                                              87
    Music and Dance                                           87
    Reader's Theater                                          88
    Puppets                                                   89
    Visual Art                                                91
    Visual Imagery                                            92
    Exploring Language                                        94
    Summary                                                   97

7.  *A Fifth-Sixth Grade Class Uses Folk Literature*          98
    Tales and Totem Poles                                     98
    Understanding the Story                                  105
    Reinforcing Understanding                                105
    Writing with Folk Literature                             107

*A Guide to Recommended Folk Literature for Children*        111

*Appendix A*                                                 161
    Folk Literature by Region and Culture                    161

*Appendix B*                                                 169
    Native American Cultural and Language Related Groups     169

*Appendix C*                                                 175
    Idea Webs for Sharing Folk Literature                    175

*References*                                                 179

*Index*                                                      183

*About the Author*                                           190

# Preface

In the four years since the first edition of *Fairy Tales, Fables, Legends, and Myths* was published, we have seen exciting changes in classrooms. More and more teachers are using literature and real-life experiences in teaching, reading, writing, and all the content subjects. As a result, they are enjoying their teaching more but are looking for guidance in selecting what is best within this broad spectrum of possibilities. I hope that this book can offer both background material and relevant teaching ideas that are adaptable to any classroom.

I am convinced that teachers make a difference in the development of lifelong readers. Teachers enthusiastically sharing books stimulate a love of reading and an appreciation of good literature.

This text focuses on folk literature, which is particularly noteworthy for capturing the interest of a wide range of readers. In the numerous schools where teachers have been trying the ideas in this book, I have found children from kindergarten to middle-school age becoming more and more enthralled with the stories.

When a sixth-grader helped me take a box of books back to my car, he said, "I wish we could keep them longer. There are still good ones that I haven't had time to read." Before the folk literature study began, this boy had not been able to name five books that he had read because he really wanted to read them.

The teaching ideas and lesson strategies in this book are based on an interactive view of reading. An interactive view of reading recognizes the close relationship between reading and writing and sees them as both processes and skills. Reading is a process of constructing meaning from print, with the reader taking an active role in thinking about the message. The message is interpreted differently by each reader, because each reader brings a unique background to the text.

The communication processes of speaking, listening, reading, and writing work together to produce school learning that translates into learning for real life. Oral responding to the reading is a natural link between the reading and writing. For more information about integrating reading and writing across the curriculum, consult Frank Smith (1982) and Lucy McCormick Calkins (1986). For a theoretical explanation of reading as an interactive process, consult Louise Rosenblatt (1978, 1983) or Smith (1988).

Two questions often asked in response to theoretical information about the reading process are: How do we teach reading as a thinking process, and how do we foster interactions among the reader, the reading material, and writing? The teaching strategies in this book address those questions.

Every teaching idea in this book has been tried with children. I wish to thank the following teachers, who have shared folk literature with their classes and have shared the results with me:

Nancy DeVries Guth, formerly the sixth-grade reading teacher at Kennedy Mid School, Gallup, New Mexico, now assistant superintendent of reading and language arts, Stafford County, Virginia

John Booy, fifth- and sixth-grade teacher, Beckwith Public School, Grand Rapids, Michigan

Myra Bradford, fifth- and sixth-grade reading teacher, Highlands Middle School, Grand Rapids, Michigan

Maureen Grey, language arts consultant, Highlands Middle School, Grand Rapids, Michigan

Dennis VanAndel and staff at Rehoboth Christian School, Rehoboth, New Mexico, and Calvin College teacher education students who worked in grades K–6

Nancy Burton, Calvin College graduate student, formerly at Stepping Stones Montessori School, Grand Rapids, Michigan

Mark VanZanten and Marilyn Scott, Potters House Christian School, Grand Rapids, Michigan

Katie Afendoulis, third-grade teacher at Collins School, Forest Hills, Grand Rapids, Michigan

Mollie Carnes, second-grade teacher at Pinewood Elementary School, Jenison, Michigan

Nancy Oosterink, third-grade teacher at Sandy Hill Elementary School, Jenison, Michigan

Barbara Split, fourth-grade teacher, Grand Haven Christian School, Grand Haven, Michigan

Delores Stouwie and Sharon Pegman, teachers at Oakdale Christian School, Grand Rapids, Michigan

I would like to thank colleagues who have read the manuscript and encouraged me along the way: Adeline DeBruyn, retired first-grade teacher, and Kathryn Blok, emerita reading professor at Calvin College. I especially wish to acknowledge Patricia Cianciolo, my advisor and mentor, professor at Michigan State University.

# 1

# The Tale

Story stands at the center of language and learning. "Read me a story" is a common refrain heard today, and "tell me a story" echoes from generations past. Folktales call out to all generations to continue the tradition by both telling and reading the tales that have been collected and translated by folklore enthusiasts. A rich legacy of folk literature is available to every child. This treasure requires a caring adult to unlock the beauty and enjoyment that the stories contain. The purpose of this book is to acquaint adults with choice folk literature and to provide ideas for sharing these stories with children.

## THE IMPORTANCE OF FOLK LITERATURE FOR CHILDREN

Folk literature is worth reading just for fun. The stories contain adventure, humor, and rich language that children can enjoy. In addition, through the folktales, the reader can enter into another culture and recognize the universality of the wishes, dreams, and problems of people around the world. The structure of the tale fulfills the children's expectations. Guided reading of folk literature, directing attention to this story structure, helps the child become a better reader.

### Expressive Language

The language of the folk storyteller combines both simple statement and rich, expressive, figurative language. The beauty and richness of language found in authentic written versions of the folktales contribute to children's language development. Folk literature is full of magical language. The magic of words grows in the child who listens to stories. Even before children can read the words, they can listen to the music of language. Reading nursery rhymes to very young children gives them an introduction to literary language. Continuing the read-aloud experiences throughout childhood and adolescence provides colorful, rhythmical word pictures. Consider, for example, the prophecy in Marianna Mayer's version of *The Twelve Dancing Princesses:*[1]

> The wizened old fortune-teller's eyes burned bright, and her thin voice crooned like a haunting echo as she said, "One through twelve, like the hours on a clock, first to last, twelve daughters you have. All as beautiful as the many months of the year. They are the future!" (unpaged)

Although nine-year-olds may not understand all the words, they sense the mood of the intriguing tale and delight in the sounds of language.

Even the youngest of readers are able to use the predictable narrative patterns to develop an understanding of story ideas and the general meaning of picturesque words. They join quickly in chanting with the gingerbread boy, "Run, run as fast as you can, You can't catch me, I'm the Gingerbread Man." The simple narrative and extensive use of dialogue help interpret the imagery. If folktales are adapted for easy reading through artificial control, limiting the storyteller's vocabulary and shortening the sentences, the enjoyment and appeal of the language is lost. Consider the beginning of the French tale *Stone Soup,* retold by Marcia Brown.

> Three soldiers trudged down a road in a strange country. They were on their way home from the wars. Besides being tired, they were hungry. In fact, they had eaten nothing for two days.
> "How I would like a good dinner tonight," said the first.
> "And a bed to sleep in," said the second.
> "But all that is impossible," said the third.
> "We must march on." (p. 1)

---

1. Further information about the folktales referred to in the text is provided in A Guide to Recommended Folk Literature for Children, which follows Chapter 7.

Note the contrast in the language used in the version of *Stone Soup* in *A New Day* (Clymer et al., 1989):[2]

> Three travelers were on their way home.
> They walked through the woods.
> They walked through meadows.
> "I need to eat," said the first traveler.
> "I need to sleep," said the second traveler.
> "I need to eat and sleep," said the third traveler.
> (pp. 131–132)

Folktales contribute many words and phrases to American speech and literature. These are lost to the person who grows up without a familiarity with folk literature. Consider, for example, names given to car models to imply power, speed, and beauty: Saturn, Taurus, Mercury, and Electra all originate in Greek mythology.

Readers who have developed an appreciation for traditional literature are able to enjoy and understand modern narrative more completely. Many fantasy writers reveal their own rich background in tradition by basing their fictional kingdoms on legendary and mythical names. Welsh legends and mythology are the inspiration for Lloyd Alexander's books about the land of Prydain and for The Dark is Rising, a sequence of five novels by Susan Cooper. In *Park's Quest* by Katherine Paterson (1988), Park's intrigue with the King Arthur legends offers him relief from the very real problems he is trying to resolve. The reader who has only read contemporary novels will lack a point of reference for understanding Park.

## The Universality of the Folktale

Folktales help the young reader make sense of the world. Reading different explanations of natural phenomena and ideas clarifies the child's own views. Because folktales have many layers of meaning, readers of differing developmental levels can appreciate them. Teacher guidance enables children to interpret and evaluate the message of the storyteller.

Reading and discussing folk literature enriches the spiritual life of

2. Sources cited in the text by an author and date in parentheses or a date in parentheses may be found in the References at the back of the book.

children. They can sense the universal search for a divine being and for answers concerning the origin of the world. Virginia Hamilton's book of myths, *In the Beginning,* introduces readers to a variety of cultural beliefs and offers a forum for clarifying their own efforts at making sense of the world. A discussion of a powerful legend, such as *The Golem* by Beverly Brodsky McDermott, leads children to face the relationship between faith and the harsh realities of human limitations. *Brothers,* retold by Florence Freedman, offers children an exemplary story of sibling relationships.

Folktales demonstrate that people throughout the world share a common need for love, hope, and security and possess feelings of happiness, anger, pride, and loneliness. The universal use of humor provides funny and exciting tales, such as the animal tricksters and the silly but resourceful folk hero like the Russian Ivan, English Jack, and German Hans. At the same time, the reader becomes sensitive to the differences between cultures. The folk stories show how different peoples respond differently to emotional and environmental conditions. Respect and admiration for Native Americans grow through understanding their close relationship with the earth and their views of humans in harmony with nature as revealed in their myths and legends.

Folktales, particularly myths, provide themes for artists and sculptors. Symbolic representations of the traditional stories have told anthropologists a great deal about the ancient cultures of the world. An interest in folk literature can lead to an appreciation of art. At the same time, an interest in the paintings, sculpture, pottery, weavings, and embroidery of various cultures can motivate the viewer to read the traditional stories.

## Story Structure

Folktales possess four characteristics that help the reader assimilate them. First, the magic in the tale lies in people and creatures being shown as they really are, not as results of wishes or dreams. In fact, wishes usually are shown to be foolish, as in the Grimm Brothers' *The Fisherman and His Wife,* in which the wife's discontent causes her to lose all she gained by wishing. Second, natural wit, intelligence, and goodness generally outsmart evil, as in Molly Bang's

*Wiley and the Hairy Man,* in which the brave Wiley outwits the wicked Hairy Man. Third, the magical power is limited. It cannot change a heart or the state of the world, but only outward conditions. Cinderella's clothes and conditions are changed, not her personality or character. Finally, evil does not win, but receives its due or is recognized as evil. Sometimes this includes a harsh treatment of evil, such as in the German *Cinderella,* as retold by the Grimms.

Children who have a good sense of story structures have formed expectations for the role of characters. Nine-year-olds respond to the question, "What is a _____ usually like?" with the reply that a wolf is hungry, a fox is sly, a witch is wicked, or a fairy is kind (Applebee, 1978).

Folktale characters are drawn very clearly and generally depicted as symbols of good or evil, wisdom or foolishness, power or weakness. This polarization of characters fits into children's expectations, which have been developing since age two, through both realistic and fanciful stories. Bruno Bettelheim (1976) argues that this stock characterization helps the child comprehend the differences between reality and fantasy more readily than is possible when figures are drawn true to life. The ambiguity that characterizes real people is difficult for a child to comprehend until the child has established positive self-identification. For older children, the folktales offer lessons in character building and social development with humor rather than didactic teaching.

Plot structure in folktales generally follows clear patterns. Chronological sequence with repetitive phrases is common in nursery tales such as *Henny-Penny* by Paul Galdone and is also found in legends such as *Bringing the Rain to Kapiti Plain* by Verna Aardema and fairytales such as *The Fisherman and His Wife* by the Grimm Brothers (see Figure 1.1). Cumulative patterns build interlocking episodes, such as in *One Fine Day* by Nonny Hogrogian and *Fool of the World and the Flying Ship* by Arthur Ransome.

Most tales use a problem-solving structure, with the setting, characters, and problem clearly stated early in the story. The story then unfolds predictably, through several episodes, until the problem is solved. "The Princess and the Frog," "Sleeping Beauty," and "East of the Sun, West of the Moon" are examples of fairy tales that fit the problem-solving plot structure. These predictable plot structures

**FIGURE 1.1**    A second-grader reads a repetitive tale to kindergarten friends.

make folktales excellent models for teachers to use in guiding readers.

## ADAPTING FOLKTALES

Children deserve high standards of artistry and authenticity in folk literature. All translators and retellers of folktales for juvenile audiences make adaptations from the original source. The adaptations fit into three categories: alteration of motif, alteration of mood, or literary simplification or elaboration. Each type of adaptation must be evaluated on the basis of how accurately the retelling reflects the oral storytelling tradition, how authentically the culture of the people is preserved, and how carefully the essence of the tale has been maintained.

Motifs are altered by softening the cruelty in the tale and by creating happy or moralized endings. Characters are changed, with adults in the original tale sometimes depicted as children in the retelling, or the sex of the characters changed to include more women. Obscenities are removed, and motifs rearranged to improve the flow of the story.

Alterations of the mood of the story often take the form of softening the tale or eliminating cultural and stylistic peculiarities. In the illustrations an artist may alter the mood either intentionally or through lack of knowledge of the culture.

Literary simplification is accomplished by cutting back on description and using simplified vocabulary. Elaboration includes injecting dialogue or fleshing out a sparse story.

Some of these changes are necessary and helpful for making the tales readable by children. Other changes affect the validity of the story. The reader must decide if the version presented is indeed an authentic rendition of the oral, traditional tale.

Margaret Read MacDonald (1979) presents the following questions that a reader can ask when evaluating the quality of literary versions of folktales for children:

1. Is information given regarding the tale's source, its teller, and its collection?
2. Is the version faithful to its source? How is it adapted?
3. Does it retain pacing, flow, linguistic playfulness, and imagery of the original?
4. Is the writing of exceptional quality?
5. Does it contain ethnic content such as images, songs, and word play?
6. Are the format and illustrations artistic and appropriate?
7. Are illustrations historically and culturally accurate?
8. How does this version compare with other versions of the same tale?
9. What are the author's qualifications?
10. How do area specialists perceive this version?
11. What effect does this story have on the child? Does the story possess a depth of human feeling and the nature of joy to bring to the reader? (pp. 122–123)

The folk literature that I recommend in this book meets MacDonald's guidelines for evaluation.

## FOLKLORE CLASSIFICATIONS AND DEFINITIONS

Two kinds of folklore classifications have been universally used. Antti Aarne, a Finnish folklorist, developed a *type index* in 1910. This index assigns a type number to each tale. For example, "Cinderella" is Type 510. Stith Thompson, a folklorist from Indiana University, published a *motif index* in 1932. This breaks each tale into small units and assigns a motif number to each unit of action and each character or major subject within the tale. For example, number R221, "flight from ball," lists "Cinderella" as a tale that includes that motif. This *Motif-Index of Folk Literature,* currently published in six volumes (Thompson, 1955–1958), is accepted by folktale scholars around the world as a standard tool for classifying folktale materials.

In *The Storyteller's Sourcebook,* Margaret Read MacDonald (1982) has made a significant contribution to folk literature for children. This source, which includes all folktale titles that appeared in the editions of the *Children's Catalog* (Issacson & Bogart, 1981) published between 1971 and 1981, indexes 556 folktale collections and 389 picture books. In addition to the motif index, which is useful for finding tale variants, the source contains a tale title index, subject index, and ethnic and geographic index. This enables the teacher, librarian, or child to find tales about a given subject, the location of the collection that contains a particular story, or titles of tales from a particular ethnic or geographic area.

Folklorists and users of folklore do not always agree on definitions and classifications of the various tales. The one area of agreement is recognition that folk literature originates in the oral tradition. The stories were passed along by storytellers and then became literature when written down by a person who heard and interpreted the tale. That person is labeled the collector, translator, adapter, or reteller of the folktale.

I believe that the child reader deserves to be introduced to folk literature in as authentic a representation as possible. Therefore, the classifications and criteria developed in this book follow the standards of the American Folklore Society. The definitions are based on descriptions found in the *Standard Dictionary of Folklore, Mythology, and Legend* (Leach & Freed, 1949).

*Folktale* is an inclusive term, referring to all kinds of narrative that has its origin in the oral tradition. The *literary folktale,* or *folk litera-*

*ture,* is the tale translated and retold as based upon the storytelling characteristic of a particular cultural group.

Four types of folktales are identified throughout this book: *fairy tales, animal tales, legends,* and *myths.* These four types were chosen because they encompass the vast majority of the tales in print today for children and because they are fairly distinctive in their differences. Each type is defined and explained below.

## Fairy Tales

A fairy tale is an unbelievable tale that includes an enchantment or other supernatural elements that are clearly imaginary. It does not necessarily contain fairies, but it often has giants or witches as well as brave and timid, good and evil people. Such stories are also referred to as household tales (the German *Marchen,* or "wonder tales"). The fairy tale motifs fall within the Aarne–Thompson tale types 300 to 749. Fairy tales share characteristics, but not every fairy tale contains all the following distinctive characteristics:

> Show how people behave in a world of magic
> Often have brave heroes who rescue helpless maidens
> Contain some characters who are either all good or all bad
> Often begin with "Once upon a time" and end with "Happily ever after" or a similar convention
> Often include a task that, if completed, brings a reward
> Often include a magic object to protect or help the main character

Modern fairy tales continue to be created by authors, such as Hans Christian Andersen, Jane Yolen, and Lloyd Alexander. Since they are credited to an author and not handed down by oral tradition, they belong to the genre of modern fantasy rather than folk literature.

## Animal Tales

The animal tale is one of the oldest forms of folk literature and is found everywhere on the globe. The primary characters are animals who act like people. These stories teach about life, usually with lessons concerning personal traits and getting along with others. Animals play a major role in the religion and mythology of Native Americans. They are symbols of creating life and providing food sources for maintaining life. Native American myths and legends feature both humans and animals, often with a transformation motif. Therefore, Native American folktales often intertwine mythical and legendary motifs within an entertaining animal tale. Their stories do not fall into neatly defined types, but reflect the Native American's holistic view of life told through allegories and parables.

The form of the animal tale fits into three main categories: trickster tales, fables, and etiological (why, or pourquoi) stories.

*Trickster* tales have one central character, usually a wise trickster in animal shape. The trickster is both a creator and a clown. Sometimes he can create good things for his people, and at other times he makes incredible mischief. John Bierhorst (1990) describes the classic trickster as greedy, vain, and pretentious but often a gifted shaman. The trickster animal is especially recognized and revered in Native American cultures. The exploits and power of the coyote are known from Alaska to the Southwest and among some tribes from the Pacific to the Atlantic. However, many tribes have other tricksters as well. Richard Erdoes (1984), a Native American folktale collector, reported a Sioux medicine man as saying, "Coyote, Iktome, and all clowns are sacred. They are a necessary part of us. A people who have so much to cry about as Indians do also need their laughter to survive" (p. 336).

In some cultures, the animal character will assume a human shape at times. For example, Anansi, the African spider, is Spider Man in stories from some African locales and Granny or a young man in tales from the Antilles.

Trickster tales are usually brief and direct. The story relies on one action, a trick or joke, as the solution to a problem. However, this is not a simple solving of a problem. The climax of a trickster tale is an unusual solution requiring admirable mental prowess. The story ends in a clever way, often with a surprising element that entertains or amuses the reader. The special quality of the ending makes the trickster tale memorable.

Listed here are the specific animal heroes of various cultural groups.

| TRICKSTER | LOCATION OR GROUP OF PEOPLE |
| --- | --- |
| Badger | Japan |
| Br'er Rabbit | Southern African Americans |
| Coyote | North American Native Americans; primarily in Canada and western United States |
| Fox | Russia; Eastern Europe; Gran Chaco region of South America |
| Manabozho, Rabbit | Native Americans in Great Lakes Region and central woodlands of the Southeast |
| Raven | Innuits; northwest Native Americans |
| Sioux SpiderMan, Iktome | Sioux tribe |
| Spider | West Africa; Antilles |
| Turtle, terrapin, or tortoise | North and West Africa; Northeast Native Americans |
| Wolf, Kauyumari | Central America |
| Zomo, hare | Africa |

*Fables* are brief animal stories with a specific lesson, generally stated at the beginning or end. Often one animal depicts the good traits and one depicts the evil. The animals are not named or developed beyond the single purpose of the tale. The fable appears to be a simple tale, but the compressed narrative reveals many layers of meaning. Two major collections of fables are the Jataka tales from Eastern culture and Aesop's fables from Western culture.

Jataka tales, recorded as early as 500 B.C., are moralistic lessons in which the Buddha is reincarnated as one of several animals, generally a lamb, deer, or crane. The philosophy taught in the Jataka tales involves recognizing the importance of the individual and the need to accept and understand the realities of life. Traits of cooperation, friendship, respect, responsibility, and ecological concern are emphasized. In English translations many of the morals and teaching verses are eliminated.

Aesop's fables are associated with a Greek slave, Aesop, who allegedly lived in Asia Minor about 600 B.C. The lessons of Aesop's fables are directed toward manipulating external forces and controlling or overcoming enemies.

*Etiological,* or *pourquoi,* animal tales explain the origin of certain characteristics of animals and were written to entertain. In contrast to legend, the pourquoi tales were not believed to be true. One can find many explanations for why the bear has a stumpy tale or why mosquitoes buzz in people's ears. The element of trickery is essential to the plot of this form of animal tale. The pourquoi form is often emulated by authors of invented stories, such as Rudyard Kipling (1902/1972) in his famous "Just So" stories.

## Legends

Legends are folktales told as fact and presumably believed by the storyteller. They are set in historic time and place, in a recognizable world. The nature of the tale can be sacred or secular, and it is often concerned with changes in creation, transformation of humans and animals, or heroic deeds. A legend can be explanatory or historic. The principal characters are humans, animals acting like humans, and supernatural creatures. A legend will often state a natural or historical fact, and then proceed to prove the fact through drawing erroneous conclusions. People in legends are concerned about results of the conflict of natural phenomena.

Legendary characters have their origin among the folk, handed down in the oral tradition. In contrast, some alleged American folk heroes have been deliberately invented. Consequently, stories about these heroes are classified as modern fantasy rather than folk literature. Paul Bunyan was created in 1914 by an advertising man, W. B. Laughhead, as a promotional figure for the Red River Lumber Company. Pecos Bill, a legendary cowboy, and Joe Magarac, a steelworker, were both invented by magazine writers in the early 1900s. Although the name Johnny Appleseed originated from a real person, John Chapman, the attributes credited to him and incidents related in the Johnny Appleseed stories were fabricated.

## Myths

Myths are folktales told as fact that develop a theory of the origin of the world and of humanity. Myths are set in a remote past, in which gods lived on the earth and humans had not yet developed an understanding of the arts and customs of life. The nature of the tale is sacred, concerned with the creation of the world and origins of natural events. The principal characters are deities and supernatural powers, often with human attributes. In some cultures, myths and legends are combined into one category, since both types of tales are presumed true by historic storytellers. The Native Americans maintain a clear distinction between these two types of folktales, based primarily on setting. The comparison of traits in legends and myths in Figure 1.2 includes criteria from the *Standard Dictionary of Folklore, Mythology, and Legend* (Leach, 1949).

## PREVIEW

In the following chapters, both background information and lesson ideas are presented to help adults share folk literature with children. The goal of every lesson is to heighten the appreciation of the stories and the ability to read. The lessons should be viewed as examples, not as prescriptions, and the teacher can adapt ideas from the model to fit a particular class. The teaching ideas are applicable to other genres of literature as well, and the reading strategies can be used in any literature-based reading program. Appendix C contains idea webs that offer a framework for integrating various aspects of teaching with folk literature. The webs are intended as models to

**FIGURE 1.2** Characteristics of myths and legends.

|  | **MYTHS** | **LEGENDS** |
|---|---|---|
| TELLER'S BELIEF | Told as fact | Told as fact |
| SETTING | Remote past<br>Gods living on<br>    earth | Historic time<br>    & place<br>Recognizable world |
| NATURE OF TALE | Sacred<br>Creation of world<br>Origins of natural<br>    events | Sacred or secular<br>Changes in creation<br>Shape changing<br>Heroic deeds |
| PRINCIPAL CHARACTERS | Deities<br>Supernatural powers | Humans or animals<br>    acting like humans |

encourage teachers to organize their own related ideas within their particular classroom setting.

The folktales presented in this book are exemplary stories from many world cultures. Included in A Guide to Recommended Folk Literature for Children, which follows Chapter 7, are the folktales in the lessons plus many more that meet the criteria for excellence of literary versions. The books in the Guide are listed by region or culture in Appendix A.

Children who learn to read through folk literature have the opportunity to become lifetime readers, understand other people, and appreciate other cultures. The teachers who have been involved in trying the teaching ideas presented here have reported that they themselves as well as their pupils have experienced a new excitement in reading.

# 2

# Folk Literature in Multicultural Education

Global understanding is nurtured by reading folk literature. If you truly wish to understand the people of the world, you must read their stories—the stories handed down from generation to generation. Getting to know people through their stories offers the personal dimension that makes the people real. People throughout the world are more alike than different. Reading the folktales of each country studied in school helps learners recognize the universal desire for humor, for establishing standards of behavior, and for finding answers to puzzling questions about the world. They will see how people everywhere use stories to teach their children and to entertain one another. Stories help reduce stereotypes already held by the children. In one sixth grade, when the teacher began a study of Russian folktales, a boy was overheard muttering, "I don't want to hear a story about Russia." Three days later, he told me, an observer, that he had just read "a neat book from Russia, *Three Rolls and One Doughnut*" (by Mirra Ginsburg). His apparent negative attitude about a Russian story had disappeared.

## THE MANY CULTURES IN AMERICA

Multicultural studies promote a better understanding of our own country. Native Americans, immigrants from around the world, and storytellers from regional cultures provide a mosaic of folklore. In

*15*

*The Rainbow People,* Lawrence Yep provides a picture of Chinese culture as it developed in California with the immigrants in the 1800s. He recalls, "When my father picked fruit in the Chinese orchards near Sacramento, the workers would gather in the shack after a hot, grueling workday; one of the ways that the old-timers would pass the time before sleep came was to tell stories" (p. x). Before his book was published in 1989, Chinese-American tales were virtually unknown outside of their local communities.

Appalachian tales as told by Richard Chase in *Grandfather Tales* and *The Jack Tales* reflect the local color, sense of humor, and dialect of the mountain folk in variants of English fairy tales and legends. Willian Hooks has told Appalachian variants of folktales that came to Appalachia with the early English, Scottish, and Irish settlers more than three centuries ago. Many years of storytelling have added local color and regional language. Folklorists, such as Gerald Milnes, are contributing to folk literature by publishing the rhymes and stories of the mountain people.

A few culturally rich Creole tales are reaching the national market, such as *The Talking Eggs* retold by Robert SanSouci.

## African American Folktales

Virginia Hamilton provides a legacy of African American tales collected in *The People Could Fly.* These tales combine the memories that the slaves took with them from Africa and their experiences as slaves torn from their culture and social groups. The stories they told featured animals with the characteristics of the people of the plantation, tales of magic, fantasy escapes, and supernatural happenings. Hamilton refers to the tales as "a celebration of the human spirit" (p. xii).

*The Knee-High Man* and *Tales of Uncle Remus* by Julius Lester are excellent collections of animal stories retold with vitality and humor. Both Hamilton and Lester contribute a personal voice that brings to life the unique culture the Africans brought to this country. Their retelling of the stories can aid all children today in understanding African Americans.

Ashley Bryan captures the voice of Africans in his skillful use of alliteration and interior rhyme in his collections of African tales, such as *Lion and the Ostrich Chicks* and *The Ox of the Wonderful Horns.* He works from the sparse story motifs found in anthropologists' collections. He has spent time in Africa to capture the feel of the land and the culture. His illustrations are based on his study of the wood sculpture, masks, and rock painting of African folk art. He does not emulate art from one tribe but rather is influenced by the styles and symbols of various tribes. He writes (Bryan, 1990):

> African tales are a beautiful means of linking the living Africa, past and present, to our own present. What the African sees in his world, the questions he asks, the things that he feels and imagines, have all found their way into our stories. (unpaginated)

## Mexican American Folktales

For most Mexican Americans, myths, folklore, and legends are found only in archives. The tales of Mexico and Central America came from the old Indian tribes and spoke of the beliefs of the Indians before the Spanish introduced Christianity. The people worshiped the elements of rain, sun, wind, and fire. Their gods, especially Quetzalcoatl and Tezcatlipoca, were violent and demanded human sacrifices. The Spanish missionaries recorded the myths to study the language and to refute the native beliefs. Consequently, the Indians hid the traditional stories for fear of ridicule and giving their communities a bad name (Bierhorst, 1990). In Mexico today some affirm their Spanish heritage and keep their Indian roots concealed. Others celebrate their Indian heritage and embrace the Indian art, architecture, history, and mythology of their nation's culture.

The tales that are translated into English for children are generally the narratives called *cuentos,* tales told for entertainment and for teaching the young. Some of the *cuentos* are taken from the basic Indian myths from pre-Columbian times, and others are from a new lore that is essentially Christian but also reinforces Indian values. *Spirit Child,* translated by John Bierhorst, and *The Lady of Guadaloupe,* retold by Tomie dePaola, are examples of the latter type of lore. *The Old Lady Who Ate People,* translated by Francisco Hinajosa, and *Why Corn Is Golden,* retold by Vivien Blackmore, are examples of basic Indian stories.

Trickster tales are popular in Mexico and Central America. Stories in which Rabbit outwits Coyote are often told, and the Tar Baby story is a favorite in southern Mexico and Guatemala. Although those stories are of European origin, they are valued as ancient narratives by the storytellers. A native Central American hero is the Huichol trickster-god, Kauyumari, the wolf. Wolf plays a role in a cycle of creation stories but to date has not appeared in children's folk literature.

## Native American Culture

Today there is a renewed interest in learning about the culture of the people who lived in North America before the Europeans arrived, and many school districts include the study of local Native Americans in their curriculum. All of the Native American tribes have an oral tradition of myths, legends, and animal tales. Indian tribes can be worlds apart in many cultural ways, but a common characteristic is a reverence and respect for the earth. Since this is a common theme in them, Native American tales can be used effectively to introduce earth science lessons. The relationship between humans and nature is the center of a valuable teacher resource, *Keepers of the Earth,* by Michael Caduto and Joseph Bruchac. The authors use Native American tales to introduce each topic and present activities and teaching ideas.

Anthropologists and folklore collectors have been collecting Native American narratives ever since Christopher Columbus brought along a scribe on his second journey to America in 1493. H. R. Schoolcraft, George Baird Grinnell, Stith Thompson, and Edward Curtis are historians who stand out from among the recorders of Indian tales. These men have preserved a wealth of authentic Native American source materials. Nevertheless, many tribes, now assimilated into Anglo culture or totally annihilated, have left no written record of their stories.

Choice stories from the anthropologists' collections have been retold for children by storytellers such as John Bierhorst and Paul Goble. Goble, an Englishman, is an adopted member of the Yakima and the Oglala Sioux tribes. Before publishing his stories he makes sure that the Native Americans approve of his retelling of their tales. His brilliant paintings in the books interpret Native American art and lore and portray the spaciousness of the Great Plains. Christie Harris has provided a literary legacy of fine Canadian and Alaskan Native American tales. The expressive imagery and figurative language captures the Native American's regard for the order of nature. Harris's *Mouse Woman* and *Totem* tales can be important components of a social studies unit in the intermediate or middle-school grades.

In many areas of the country, local historical societies and state park commissions can provide information about local tribes. Often local historians have collected and published Native American stories. For example, the Mackinac Island State Park Commission has published *Lore of the Great Turtle* (Gringhuis, 1970). The Zion Natural History Association of Springdale, Utah, published *Why the North Star Stands Still and Other Indian Legends* by William R. Palmer (1978). Sourcebooks on Native Americans of the Willamette valley are available from the Mission Mill Museum Association of Salem, Oregon. For a list of Native American tribes of North America and more information about Native American cultural and language related groups, see Appendix B.

## TRANSLATION OF FOLK LITERATURE

Folk literature could not be enjoyed by American readers if the stories had not been translated. In fact, the only tales that originated in English are the English folktales and American regional and tall tales. Native Indian myths and legends were first told or written down in tribal language. Increased interest in folklore in the past decade has encouraged many language scholars to translate old tales into English for the first time.

Authentic translation requires considerable study. For example, John Bierhorst, a well-respected adapter of American Indian tales, translated *Spirit Child* into English in 1984 from Aztec Indian documents of the mid-1500s. He found the documents when he was preparing an Aztec–English dictionary. He has produced three books on the mythology of the New World (1985, 1988, 1990), which are rich sources of information about the cultural history of the people of North, Middle, and South America.

Ai-Ling Louie studied manuscripts that date back to A.D. 618–907 before translating *Yeh Shen* into English. Lynette Vuong studied several Vietnamese folktale volumes before attempting her colorful translation of *The Brocaded Slipper and Other Vietnamese Tales* in 1982. Boris Zvorykin translated four Russian fairy tales into French as a gift of gratitude for the new life he made in France in the 1920s after the Russian Revolution. The fairy tales were translated into English in 1978 and published with reproductions of the original illustrations. Verna Aardema investigates as many early translations of old African scripts as possible before beginning her versions of African tales. She incorporates ideophones from the African language to add rhythm and flavor to the story.

The reader or teller of tales can increase children's awareness that the folktales they enjoy are translated from other languages. Whenever introducing or sharing a folktale, talk about the original language of the story. References found in book prefaces or epilogues can stimulate children to embark on individual inquiries, researching the country, the language, or the act of translating. Some books, such as *Yeh Shen,* include a sample of the original language. Others, like *Korean Cinderella* by E. B. Adams and *Arroz con leche: Popular Songs and Rhymes from Latin America* by Lulu Delacre, include the original language alongside the English translation throughout the book.

The fifth–sixth grade class described in Chapter 7 was asked, "What if no one had translated these stories? Would that make a difference to you?" Typical answers were

> I'd miss the fun of reading them.
> If we read their stories [those belonging to other cultures] and like them, we will cooperate more with them because we will see that we agree with each other.
> We wouldn't learn how different people from different places teach their children. When we read them it teaches us lessons just like they taught their children lessons.
> They are of great value because they teach us why things are important and why things are the way they are.

## BOOK ILLUSTRATION AND CULTURAL UNDERSTANDING

The artistic quality of the book illustrations in much of recently published folk literature helps children visualize and understand world cultures. The artist's conception of the geographic locale of the story transmits the universality or differences among the cultures, as well as a sense of history. The artist's imaginative portrayal of legendary characters or fairy-folk stimulates the child's ability to develop visual images. Children cannot create in a vacuum and should not be limited to television images as models for creating their own imaginative worlds.

Fairy tale illustration sets the mood for the story and places the tale firmly in a historical time and place. Paul Zelinsky presents the rich, brocaded costumes of the medieval court against the cold, gray stone of a German castle in *Rumpelstiltskin*. The messenger travels through the foreboding, hilly countryside at night searching for clues to name the gold-spinner. Zelinsky offers the same traditional setting with period dress in *Hansel and Gretel,* retold by Rika Lesser. The dignity of the Grimms' *Snow White* tale has been restored by artists Nancy Burkert and Trina Hyman. They both picture the seven dwarfs as coal miners in the Black Forest of Germany, where little people worked in the low-ceiling mines where taller workers could not stand. The medieval cottage is architecturally authentic, with every detail verified from German museums. The cottage and the miners in the fairy tale are real. The make-believe objects are the magic from the castle: the mirror, the poisoned comb, and the apple, poisoned only on the red half.

Authentic illustrations allow the children to view land and castles in different countries and to sort out the real from the make-believe. English, French, and German castles pictured in "Cinderella" versions can be compared with photographs of real castles in those countries. American children tend to think that castles are part of the imaginary element of the fairy tales. A third-grade study, described in Chapter 6, includes comparing real castles with imaginary ones.

The dignity of the African American heritage is celebrated in John Steptoe's paintings in *Mufaro's Beautiful Daughters*. Inspiration for his drawings came from visiting an ancient city in Zimbabwe. The characters are portrayed with splendid self-assurance and serious concern for their fellow citizens. The countryside is lush and beautiful. His illustrations and the text make a strong statement of courage and caring that would not only impress African American readers but would offer understanding to readers of other cultural backgrounds. This book should be in every elementary school library or classroom.

Ed Young had a hard time beginning the illustrations for *Yeh Shen* by Ai-Ling Louie. Young's research of old China revealed that the Hmong people in the area where the tale originated *did not wear shoes. How could the story be authentic?* Then a librarian at the New York City library found a document with sketches of costumes and finery that the Hmong people wore at festivals. There were the brocaded slippers! The paintings immediately began to take shape, and Young set the pastel illustrations in panels like a folding painted screen, reflecting his deep feeling for his own Chinese heritage.

## INTERNATIONAL STUDIES

To fulfill the purpose of developing a global understanding of cultures, it is necessary to go beyond an occasional reading of folktales. Folk literature and other ethnic literature should become curricula material whenever subject areas address cultural similarities and differences.

A middle-school international literature unit at Fred Lynn Middle School, Prince William County, Virginia, began with readings from their large library collection of folk literature. Teachers read aloud and children read silently and orally to a partner. Cooperative learning groups were formed in which each student took a book from the same country and compared the characters, story message, illustrations, and portrayal of the country. This led to research on customs, foods, and character traits. The art teacher featured displays of art styles from countries studied and encouraged the students in a variety of art projects related to the books and the specific countries. As an outgrowth of their folk literature study, the middle schoolers planned an International Day for the entire school community. A Food Fair was organized in the school cafeteria, with parents and teachers donating a food dish from a country where they were born or had lived. A program featured students, faculty, and community members performing dances and songs from many countries. Most popular was the fashion show, with boys, girls, and teachers modeling costumes from different countries. Parents delighted in resurrecting native costumes and proudly telling their children the history behind the outfit. This information was then related to the audience during the fashion show. A fashion parade was held during the International Food Fair, where visitors could sample ethnic foods while watching the show. Every corner of the cafeteria was decorated with booths illustrating students' studies of other countries. A veritable museum of folklore included artifacts, dolls, pottery, china, sculpture, and wood carvings.

This middle-school study demonstrates the value of going beyond an introductory level of multicultural experiences. If you are just beginning to develop a multicultural curriculum, I recommend that you consult two excellent books: *Multicultural Education* by James and Cherry Banks (1989) and *Teaching Strategies for Ethnic Studies* by James Banks (1987). James Banks describes four levels of increasing involvement in multicultural considerations: the contributions approach, the additive approach, the transformation approach, and the social action approach. Each of these approaches can be enhanced through the reading of folk literature.

In the *contributions approach,* the teacher introduces ethnic heroes and cultural elements such as dances, music, and customs. An example of this would be to read *Whistle in the Graveyard,* a collection by Maria Leach, at Halloween, or to read *Yeh Shen,* translated by Ai-Ling Louie, or *Suho and the White Horse,* retold by Yuzo Otsuka, when studying China. In this first level of involvement, contributions of other cultures are limited to heroes and holidays and seldom mentioned in any other context. This is a beginning, but one must be careful that this does not become a token consideration of the mosaic of nationalities that contribute to our culture.

In the *additive approach,* content, concepts, themes, and perspectives are added to the curriculum without changing its structure. The teacher is more conscious of incorporating multicultural sources. This is an important step toward exposing children to a variety of people and points of view, because left to their own, children will select familiar stories. For example, a study of Russia would include Marcus Crouch's *Ivan* and Boris Zvorykin's *The Firebird.* Reading the introduction to *The Firebird* introduces the listener to the Russian heritage so loved by Zvorykin and reflected in the eloquent, rich illustrations. Stocking the room with folk literature from Russia and encouraging children to read these tales is a move in the right direction.

Both the contribution and additive approaches make substantive additions to a multi-ethnic classroom. As a new teacher, this may be the way to begin if your school does not have a curriculum that integrates contributions from other cultures. You are able to put ethnic content into the curriculum without restructuring it. However, one must be careful that this does not add to stereotypes. If the reader chooses only trickster books, for example, he will get a distorted view of the folk culture of Russia.

Comparing and discussing these books moves you to the third model for integration, a *transformation approach*. Here students are encouraged to view problems, themes, concerns, and concepts from the perspective of different cultural groups. This goes beyond presenting the cultural differences to understanding and appreciating that various ethnic and cultural groups have influenced, shaped, and participated in developing America into what it is today.

This means infusing the curriculum with literature that presents cultural viewpoints that can be compared and contrasted. Virginia Hamilton's *The People Could Fly* becomes part of a study of African Americans along with informational books and fiction. Textbooks and other tradebooks would be analyzed according to how clearly they depict the Americas as a multicultural society.

The fourth level of ethnic integration is the *social action approach*. Movement from the transformation approach to the social action approach is gradual. Here students are taught to become reflective social and political citizens with knowledge, values, and skills that enable them to participate in social change for the victimized and discriminated-against groups in society. The social gathering of the middle-school families at Fred Lynn School resulted from the literature study and fostered a positive community spirit.

## SUMMARY

Folk literature provides a means of understanding cultures and of moving students toward literacy in English. This chapter introduces you to the work of translators, collectors, and illustrators of folktales from the mosaic of cultures represented in America. Native American folktales play an important role in curriculum studies of local Native American tribes. The excellent artwork in children's folk literature offers a source for developing art appreciation and a visual perception of the imaginary or historic time and place.

A framework is offered for the teacher who is implementing a multicultural curriculum. Folk literature becomes a part of each of four levels of involvement (Banks & Banks, 1989). These levels are the contributions approach, additive approach, transformation approach, and social action approach.

# 3

# *Understanding the Story*

A classroom study of folk literature should begin with storytelling or reading the tales aloud. A group of children listening to and watching the storyteller follow the oral tradition begun before print was invented. Cultural groups around the world developed storehouses of tales that were told in family and clan gatherings to entertain, to explain the world around them, and to caution and teach the young.

The magic of the story is captured in the telling, and most children need this introduction before they will enjoy reading the stories themselves. Teachers in a middle school who used folk literature in their reading program reported that reading one folktale a day, or one that took two days to complete, whetted the pupils' interest. Frequently the children would select those stories to reread.

## READING ALOUD

When reading folktales aloud, teachers should take the time to stop and discuss interesting ideas, cultural differences, and the storyteller's rich use of language. The beauty and richness of language found in authentic versions of folktales contribute to children's language development. Two ways to direct the oral reading experience is by reading aloud for language response and by reading aloud for prediction.

## Reading Aloud for Language Response

A kindergarten or first-grade teacher cannot assume that all children will come to school knowing nursery tales such as "Three Billy Goats Gruff," "Gingerbread Boy," "Henny-Penny," or "The Little Red Hen." Children who do know them enjoy hearing these favorite stories again and again. Many of the folktales that please the very young child use a repetitive or a cumulative story pattern. The repetitive pattern is characterized by a refrain or the repetition of an episode. The cumulative pattern adds a new thought or episode, and then repeats what has gone before in the story. Both patterns enhance the young child's awareness of language. Young children delight in discovering a pleasing flow of language and being able to repeat the rhythmical expressions. The rhythmical pattern helps the child understand and recall the sequence and the content of the story. The framework directs the readers' attention to the next episode and helps them keep track of what has happened. When simpler words are substituted, but the anticipated patterns are broken, the story is made more difficult rather than easier to understand.

The superb telling of nursery tales by Paul Galdone uses repetition of words and phrases. The following plan utilizes this repetition to provide both enjoyment and language growth.

**LESSON OBJECTIVE:**  To develop language awareness through repetition of phrases in an enjoyable story.

**MATERIALS:**  One of Paul Galdone's books (see A Guide to Recommended Folk Literature) or another folktale with a repetitive pattern; tagboard strips with the printed refrain from the story.

**PROCEDURE:**

1. Read the story expressively.
2. After the refrain has been repeated a few times, stop just short of the next time it occurs. Ask the children to join you. If they do not respond, simply continue reading, but give auditory emphasis to the refrain.
3. The next time the refrain is repeated, stop and nonverbally indicate that the listeners may provide the next words. With some groups, this will begin spontaneously. Others will need more modeling before they are able to respond.

4. Reread the story, either at the same sitting or at another time, and place the tagboard strips in a pocketchart. This provides a speech-to-print correspondence for the nonreader and a printed version for the beginning reader. Resist the urge to use the tagboard strip at the first reading. The children who know the speech-to-print relationships will benefit, but not the ones who have not yet developed that concept.
5. As a variation of step 4, involve the children in placing the strips or reading them. Make sure that the child who needs to develop this prereading concept is an active participant.

Language patterns assist experienced readers as well as beginners. Folktales such as *Tikki Tikki Tembo* by Arlene Mosel, *Why Mosquitoes Buzz in People's Ears* and *Bringing the Rain to Kapiti Plain,* both retold by Verna Aardema, contain repetitive and cumulative patterns. When reading these and similar tales, elicit response from the listeners to emphasize the language patterns.

## Reading Aloud for Predictions

Asking children to predict what they think the story will be about involves the listener as an active participant in the story sharing. As the story unfolds, the listeners are able to prove or change their predictions. This establishes a purpose for reading and a thoughtful approach to understanding the story.

**LESSON OBJECTIVE:** To encourage listeners to predict the turn of events in the story and to recognize the need for information in making a valid prediction.

**MATERIAL:** Since all folktales are predictable to varying degrees, select a tale that fits the level of thinking of your children.

Examples for primary grades: *The First Morning* by Margery Bernstein; *Who's in Rabbit's House?* by Verna Aardema; *Fin M'Coul* by Tomie dePaola.

Examples for intermediate grades: *The Dancing Granny* by Ashley Bryan; *Sunflight* by Gerald McDermott; *Liang and the Magic Paintbrush* by Demi.

**PROCEDURE:**
1. Read the story aloud and elicit predictions, beginning with the title or the opening sentences.

**2.** Stop reading at a planned spot, and ask if any predictions have already come true or if the listener wants to change a prediction. If they wish to change, expect them to give their reasons, based on what they have heard so far in the story.

**3.** Ask the listeners to respond to questions such as

   **a.** Why don't you know if your prediction is true?

   **b.** What other information do you need?

   **c.** Do you want to keep your prediction or change it? Why?

After the children become adept at making and verifying predictions from folktales, guide prediction practice with other types of writing, such as news stories and editorials. This will help readers understand that what they learn from story reading is applicable to other kinds of literature and to expository writing.

## Children Reading Aloud

It is important for children to develop fluent oral reading. This permits them to communicate what they have read to others clearly and expressively. It requires practice and teacher guidance. Until children become clear, fluent readers, consider having them read to small groups of classmates rather than the whole class. This provides both a more comfortable listening experience and more comfortable reading practice.

The expressive reading by the teacher provides a model for the child reader. Since you have read to them frequently before asking them to share their story, they will be ready to follow your model. First, allow the children to read the story silently before attempting to read it aloud. Encourage them to practice the expression they will use for the characters' voices and the rhythm of the language.

When the child is ready to share a tale, the audience should be prepared. Discuss together how and why a person should listen to a reader. The children will probably offer more suggestions than you would make. At times involve the listeners in evaluating the reading. Prepare a checklist for them to mark with items such as:

   Did the reader keep you interested in the story?
   Could you hear the rhythm or repetitions in the story clearly?
   Did the reader vary his or her tone of voice?

Could you tell when a different character was talking?
How did the story make you feel?

See Chapter 6 for creative activities with oral reading, such as readers theater and dramatics.

## GUIDING READING COMPREHENSION

Although the origin of folktales is in the oral tradition, added appreciation of the stories develops when the reader understands the story while reading silently. The teacher's role is to make these stories available, in the classroom or library, and to guide the readers toward an understanding of what they read.

Folktales can be used with children of all ages because of the tales' many layers of meaning. The subtle messages that delight the older child are not picked up by the younger reader, but that does not lessen appreciation of the story. The experienced teacher adjusts the lessons to challenge children at their appropriate developmental level. For example, consider the different responses given by primary school children and older intermediates to *Baba Yaga* by Ernest Small. The younger child expects Marusia to get away from the witch because of the predictability of the fairy tale: Children always escape the witch! The older child responds to the theme and expects Marusia to be released because of the message: Evil cannot win in the presence of love. A teacher must strive for a balance that avoids either making a lesson too easy or assuming that the children have more knowledge than they really do.

For some of the strategies described in this chapter, alternatives for different age levels are given, but generally that decision must be left to the discretion of the teacher. Two methods for guiding silent reading are described: story mapping and the directed reading-thinking activity.

### Story Mapping

A story map is a graphic display of the logical organization of events and ideas important in the unfolding of the story. Use of story mapping develops comprehension by directing the reader's attention to the story structure.

The teacher must become proficient at mapping stories before introducing the process to children. During preparation for group mapping, the teacher should devise questions that will aid the reader in organizing and integrating the story content and should avoid questions that simply test recall or focus on assessing literal meaning. Questions should consider the overall concept of the story rather than isolated items in the story. The form of the map should reflect the story structure. For example, the mapping chart shown in Figure 3.1 fits the plot resolution structure which is common in fairy tales, fables, myths, and legends.

**LESSON OBJECTIVE:**   To help children recognize the structure of a story.
**MATERIAL:**   The folktale that you have selected, such as *Fin M'Coul* by Tomie dePaola; chart paper or newsprint; story map outlines for individuals (optional).

**FIGURE 3.1**   Story mapping chart.

```
TITLE OF STORY


    SETTING                   Where
                              When


    CHARACTERS                Who


    PROBLEM


    ACTION                    1
                              2
                              3   (as many as needed)

    RESOLUTION
```

**PROCEDURE:**

1. Reproduce the story map outline on a large piece of newsprint, so that it is visible for all. (See Figure 3.2) Each child can have a copy to fill out while you are writing on the large chart.

2. Involve the pupils in answering questions about setting and characters, while filling out the map. When time or place is not stated, inferential thinking is needed. Demonstrate how clues to determining setting can be picked up through pictures, dialogue, or particular phrases. For the first mapping experience with young children, select a story that gives all the setting information very clearly. Note how Tomie dePaola begins his retelling of *Fin M'Coul:*

    In olden times,
    when Ireland's glens and woods
    were still filled with fairies and leprechauns,
    giants too lived on that fair Emerald Isle. (p.1)

    Here you have all the information concerning setting in the opening lines.

3. Continue to guide, discussing how to state the problem as simply as possible and selecting the actions. At first you state why each

**FIGURE 3.2**
Fourth-graders map a story they have read with their teacher.

action is chosen. Then, once the children recognize that each action must work toward solving the problem, they can say why each action is chosen. You can demonstrate that connection by comparing the contributing actions with minor episodes that do not advance the story line.

4. Guide the reader to state the resolution in key words chosen from the story. Asking questions such as "When did you realize the problem was being solved?" accentuates the thought process involved. Include "what if" questions if you wish to discuss alternative ways of solving the problem.

Several modeling experiences may be necessary before the readers can use story mapping as a tool for better understanding of the story. Moving from teacher-led mapping, to small groups, to partners, and then to independent mapping makes the experience more enjoyable and provides the necessary practice to ensure success.

Story maps can vary from the basic structure described above to emphasize parts of the story or to fit the understanding level of the reader or listener. Third-graders in Katie Afendoulis's class recorded their impressions of "Cinderella" stories when they read them independently (Figure 3.3). Later the individual accounts were compared for similarity and differences (see Chapter 4).

They can also be used with young children in preparation for the time when they will be able to read on their own. Familiarity with story structure is an important part of emerging literacy. Two kindergarten teachers at Oakdale Christian School, Grand Rapids, Michigan, used story map variants to assist in sequential recall and use of story patterns.

A story staircase helped Sharon Pegman's kindergartners retell the repetitive story *Anansi and the Moss-Covered Rock* (retold by Eric Kimmel). A group of children drew animals, modeled after Mrs. Pegman's chart (Figure 3.4), and dictated the story sequence to fill a large paper. The graphic form of the steps guided their memory of the sequence of events. Mrs. Pegman wrote what the child dictated under the step. At the first-grade level, children could write it themselves, using spelling appropriate to their developmental level.

The structure of *Once a Mouse* by Marcia Brown is a perfect fit for a circle map (Figure 3.5). Delores Stouwie's kindergartners rehearsed the flow of story events by manipulating large, freehand-

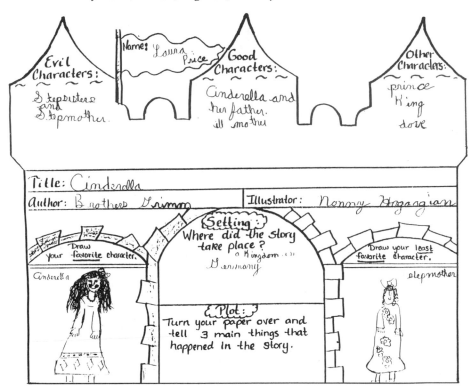

**FIGURE 3.3**  Third-grader, Grand Rapids, Michigan records her impressions of a fairy tale she has read.

drawn pictures patterned from the book illustrations and placed on magnetic backing. A large circle was drawn on the chalkboard. In a clockwise sequence, the story was mapped out by the children. Several children noticed that the classroom clock had the same formation. In a short time, the children were able to sequence the story without prompting, using the figures. In the process, they learned about big and little and decided that big was not always better. Mrs. Stouwie reported that this was an exciting way to make a story concrete.

For older children, the graphic plan could take the form of a flowchart or a web showing relationships of components of the story. With each type of map, modeling by the teacher is important because knowledge of how to follow one structure may not transfer

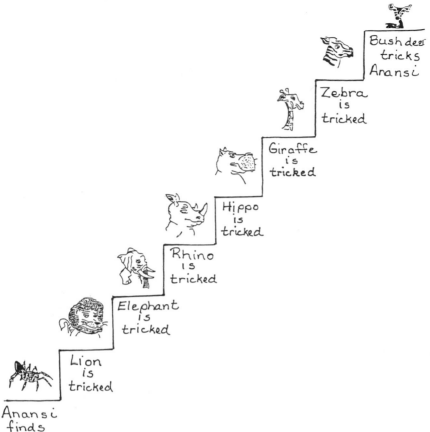

**FIGURE 3.4** Kindergartners follow the story structure of *Anansi and the Moss-Covered Rock* with a story staircase. Illustrations by Nate Pegman.

to another form. All variants of story mapping are worthy of regular repetition so that they become a tool for better story understanding.

## Directed Reading-Thinking Activity

A second strategy for guiding readers to general comprehension is the directed reading-thinking activity (Stauffer, 1980). This activity is similar to the strategy used in the reading-aloud-for-

**FIGURE 3.5**    A circular map helps children recall the storyteller.

predictions lesson, but now the child reads silently. The predict–read–prove sequence gives a purpose for reading and engages the reader in thinking about the broad and deep meaning of the story content. The practice in making predictions while listening prepares the reader for making predictions before and during silent reading.

**LESSON OBJECTIVE:**    To guide readers to general comprehension.
**MATERIAL:**    Multiple copies of a folktale that pupils can read. (Many basal readers have adaptations of folktales that would be appropriate for this activity.)

**PROCEDURE:**

1. Meet with a small group of pupils.
2. Predict—elicit predictions based on the title and pictures.
3. Read—ask pupils to read to a certain point.
4. Prove—discuss whether or not the predictions are coming true and whether more information is needed.
5. Continue this sequence, with teacher-selected stopping places for discussion.

## VOCABULARY DEVELOPMENT

Words must communicate a message to the listener or reader in order to be understood and remembered. The vocabulary strategies in this chapter are based on three assumptions concerning language development. The first is that children's language develops naturally in an adequate learning environment. This environment includes reading to children and discussing stories they have read, teaching language use within the context of the story, and providing time for silent reading.

Second, a child's understanding of words exceeds production. Therefore, vocabulary development grows through experiences that allow the child to assimilate the meaning of words by listening to stories and discussing the author's use of words to express ideas. Both oral and silent reading practice provides the repetition needed for ownership of the literary vocabulary.

Third, language learning never ends. People are social beings who communicate to one another primarily through talking, listening, reading, and writing. Effective communication requires lifelong learning. Messages can be interpreted at different levels of complexity. Folk literature uses language that has layers of meaning. The young child is able to assimilate as much as his or her developmental level will allow. The older child can read the same tale and understand a deeper meaning, especially if that reader is guided in an understanding of picturesque or metaphoric language. Both the younger and the older child will benefit from the guidance of a teacher in developing their optimum levels of vocabulary understanding.

## Oral and Written Context

Able readers enrich their vocabularies greatly in independent reading by interpreting new words in context. Teachers can guide young readers to develop the habit of scrutinizing the context of unfamiliar words and phrases so that the reader can make sensible guesses, or predictions, about the meaning of the unknown words.

Vocabulary consists of various kinds of language:

> Plot-carrying words, which must be known in order to understand the story line
>
> Descriptive words, which indicate the author's style and set the mood
>
> Concept-carrying words, which require adequate background knowledge for understanding the theme of the story

While children usually experience little difficulty with plot-carrying and descriptive words, they may need help with concept-carrying ones. Difficult concept-carrying words will need prior explanation, or may be an indication that the tale is more appropriate for older children. For example, cautionary tales often deal with character traits. Many of those tales use humor to get the message across to the reader. *The Lazies* by Mirra Ginsburg was a favorite of sixth-graders who were studying folktales. However, to truly enjoy the humor, the reader had to know the meaning of such words as *shrewdness, laziness,* and *idler*. When children respond to a story by saying "I didn't get it" or "The story doesn't make sense," it means they generally are unable to understand the concept-carrying vocabulary.

In the same sixth grade, many children were attracted to Jan Carew's *The Third Gift*. However, few would finish it. Finally, one boy brought it to the teacher and asked if she would read it to them, because it seemed so good but was hard to understand. The teacher read it, stopping frequently to ask the listeners what a particular phrase meant, such as "through endless seasons of waxing and waning moons" (p. 10). When the sixth-graders heard the expressions in context, they were able to understand them. The difficult language was easier to understand because now, in addition to the written context, the listener could use cues of intonation, stress, pitch, and juncture to help conceptualize the meaning. The discussions that followed demonstrated a rich understanding and appreciation for the life views of the Juba people. Analyzing the context helped the reader interpret the message.

LESSON OBJECTIVE: To help the reader unlock the message by making sensible guesses from the context.

MATERIAL: *The Third Gift* by Jan Carew; transparencies and overhead projector.

PROCEDURE:

1. After reading *The Third Gift* aloud, show the following difficult passages on an overhead projector.

   > Amakosa summoned the elders of the clan to a palaver. It was a time when endless seasons of drought and dust were scattering the Jubas. (p. 7)

   Lead the group in analyzing why they were not able to understand this.

   a. What didn't you understand when you tried to read this alone? (Underline those words.)

   b. What made it possible to understand it when you heard it?

2. If all the responses lead to the oral communication, point out that written messages can be harder to understand because there are less clues for finding the meaning. Then demonstrate how readers can examine the other words in the passage. Draw arrows to the words, and suggest questions that the readers should ask themselves to determine the meaning. For example, if *palaver* is the unknown word, underline it on the transparency and ask the following questions:

   a. Do the surrounding words tell you enough for you to guess the meaning of the word?

   b. If not, what should you do: Skim to find *palaver* in another sentence and try again, or look it up in the dictionary?

3. Present a new passage on the transparency, such as

   > One evening, when the gloaming was giving way to starlight and pale lightnings. (p. 10)

   Lead readers to verbalize what they would look for and think about when deciding on the meaning of the passage. Repeat the process used with *palaver,* asking which word to underline and

where to draw arrows for supporting clues. Suggest that the reader say a difficult passage quietly aloud if oral clues help.
4. Allow silent reading time, during which the readers are encouraged to notice what they do when they read a word or encounter an idea that is not clear. Take time to discuss their findings after the silent reading session.

As a reinforcing activity, post a chart in the room on which children can write unusual words in the context in which they found them.

Folktales that have been retold with the flavorful language of the native country introduce children to many literary words that they would not hear in other settings. If interest in language has been developed, children will be able to understand the unusual words from the context, and simple easy-to-read versions will not be necessary.

## Figurative Language

The young reader needs to understand idiomatic and figurative expressions. Understanding figurative language leads children to create their own fresh metaphors and make better use of common, or frozen, metaphors. Similes, metaphors, and idioms are found in nearly every child's story, both in basal readers and in children's literature. Unless figurative speech is taught, children tend to misunderstand the message of the author.

Common idioms used by a particular group are difficult for the child from a different cultural background, or for the child who comes from a home where the family seldom converses. The idiom of folktales from other countries will be new to most children and offers a common ground to begin teaching how to interpret idioms.

LESSON OBJECTIVE:    To recognize idioms as expressions peculiar to a language or dialect of a region or class of people, with a meaning different from the literal; to be able to interpret idioms in independent reading.

MATERIAL:    *When Shlemiel Went to Warsaw and Other Stories* by Isaac Bashevis Singer; transparencies; chart paper.

**PROCEDURE:**
1. Read "Shrewd Todie & Lyser the Miser" for enjoyment (p.3).
2. Explain that much of the humor in the story depends on under-standing the idioms. If necessary, define *idiom* and introduce it as a new word to be remembered.
3. Show the prepared transparency with an idiom from the story:
   > It was said of Todie that if he decided to deal in candles the sun would never set. (p.3)
4. Discuss what the literal meaning would be: What clues about the literal meaning help you decide on the intended meaning?
5. Note that idioms can be categorized by their main source of comparison: animals, color, clothing, food, plants, the solar system, or parts of the body. Have the children decide on the category for that idiom. Compare the meaning within that category to the context of the idiom.

As a reinforcing activity, prepare a chart with the names of possible categories for the source of the idiom. Encourage the children to categorize idioms that they meet in their reading, using steps 4 and 5 to guide them.

Metaphors and similes can be taught in a similar manner. Similes are the easiest to understand, since the clue word *like* or *as* is used, and young children can be taught to understand and use similes effectively. Metaphors, with the implied comparison, are more difficult to understand, and children often get incorrect visual pictures because of this misunderstanding. Lifting these phrases out of a story and examining them together orally leads children to enjoy those expressions rather than skip over them. Such direct instruction in figurative language exerts a powerful influence on children in developing their own understanding and use of idioms, similes, and metaphors.

Sixth-graders were asked to offer their written explanations for the following figurative expressions they found in their independent folktale reading:

> "He's a wolf in sheep's clothing" (from Aesop's fables). *Child's explanation:* He's like a private agent.
> "Don't count your chickens before they hatch" (from Aesop's

fables). *Children's explanation:* Like, you're mowing a lawn and you have the money spent before you get it.—Like my sister had five kittens and five people who wanted them. Then one died.

"My heart is breaking with grief" (from *The Loon's Necklace* by William Toye). *Child's explanation:* I'm so sad that there's a lump in my throat.

## SUMMARY

An enthusiastic and knowledgeable teacher can enhance pupils' understanding of a story in numerous ways. Teaching strategies in this chapter are designed to assist the teacher in helping children enjoy and appreciate stories. Suggestions for teacher reading aloud include reading for language response and reading for predictions. Guiding silent reading includes eliciting predictions through a directed reading–thinking activity and mapping based on the structure of the story. The maps are modeled with the children through reading aloud and group participation. Maps take the form of a graphic outline, circle, staircase, flowchart, or timeline. Children create their own forms for recalling the story structure. Repeated experiences with such visual representation help develop story comprehension.

Vocabulary lessons are based on the assumption that vocabulary develops in a natural environment, that children's listening vocabulary is larger than their speaking vocabulary, and that language learning never ends. Vocabulary strategies are presented for the oral and written context of the unknown word or phrase and for figurative language interpretation.

# 4

# Critical Reading

The child who becomes a lifelong reader is one who has developed an appreciation for reading. Appreciation is enhanced by the ability to read critically. Critical reading is a process of reconstructing the meaning of the printed message through analysis, synthesis, and evaluation. It is a complex skill that requires direct instruction, practice, and experience, plus the ability to sustain a questioning attitude toward the narrative. The ability to read critically should become as much a part of the reading act as general comprehension or word recognition. Actually, general understanding and critical reading happen concurrently. Nevertheless, to be able to read critically is a learned procedure. It does not happen automatically or intuitively for most readers. The goal of teaching critical reading is to develop a discerning reader, not a literary critic.

Teaching critical reading begins with oral interaction. Talking together about ideas in books gives the children practice in thinking aloud. The teacher is the key in guiding students toward reflective reading rather than merely grasping the facts explicitly stated in the text. Questions that lead to critical thinking and modeling topic talk require careful teacher planning.

Folktales provide excellent stories for the teacher to read while modeling strategies for critical reading. Because they are multileveled, they can be interpreted at a level appropriate to the reader. The direct plot, clear-cut characterization, and recognizable theme make interpreting and evaluating the message of the storyteller easier than in fantasy and contemporary fiction.

Lessons in this section are examples used for teaching four specific critical reading strategies. The strategies can be adapted for any other aspect of critical reading that you plan to teach. They engage the reader in developing the ability to classify; to compare relevant information and draw conclusions from those comparisons; to make judgments concerning the interpretation of story; and to recognize the theme of a story and evaluate the effectiveness of its presentation. These strategies need not be taught in the order presented. Although thinking-reading skills are interrelated, one does not have to be mastered in order for the reader to understand the other.

In each lesson, I recommend that pupils jot down notes during the modeling and the reflective parts of the lesson. Getting children into the habit of writing down what they are thinking about treats writing as a natural part of learning rather than a final product. They can use either their journals or separate "jotting books" in which they record ideas from various content areas. This writing is a tool for learning and should not be graded. It can be used by pupils later to review the reading strategies they have learned.

## CLASSIFYING TYPES AND CHARACTERISTICS

Classifying folktales gives the reader a framework for learning how to categorize ideas into groups and subgroups. Folk historians and users do not agree on folktale classifications. Many stories include elements of both legends and myths, as well as some element of fairy tales. Animals are main characters in much folklore—not only in that classified as animal tale. This very arbitrary nature of the categorizing makes folk literature appropriate for using with readers who are developing the skill of recognizing similar characteristics and using that skill to group ideas. It helps free the reader from the mindset that everything in print is either right or wrong. The classifier must weight the evidence and decide on which category the story fits best. Teaching suggestions are given for developing the background necessary for categorizing fairy tales, animal tales, legends, and myths.

### Fairy Tales

**LESSON OBJECTIVE:**   To introduce fairy tales.
**MATERIALS:**   "Vassilissa the Fair" (*The Firebird*, by Boris Zvorykin) is a good tale to use for modeling by teachers in grades 4 through 6

with children who already know "Cinderella." It is a Russian version of "Cinderella" with added motifs that demonstrates all the characteristics of a good fairy tale. For the younger child, a version of Perrault's French *Cinderella* will be the most familiar story. Teacher-made poster with the characteristics of a fairytale. Notebooks in which children will record their own thoughts.

**PROCEDURE:**

1. Read the story for sheer enjoyment of the tale.
2. Present a poster of the fairy tale characteristics listed in Chapter 1.
   Fairy tales:
   Show how people behave in a world of magic
   Often have brave heroes who rescue helpless maidens
   Contain some characters who are either all good or all bad
   Often begin with "Once upon a time" and end with "Happily ever after"
   Often include a task that, if completed, brings a reward
   Often include a magic object to protect or help the main character
3. Guide a discussion with the students as they find evidence within the tale you read for as many of the characteristics as they can. The following questions are presented as examples that can elicit thoughtful responses from the students. While the questions are being answered, encourage the children to write down either their own idea or one that they hear from their classmates.
   **a.** Who was human in this story?
   **b.** Was there a brave hero? Explain (Vasilissa is a brave heroine, and a discussion will probably ensue as to whether or not the czar was a hero in this story).
   **c.** Were some characters all good and some all bad? Explain your choice.
   **d.** What were the task and the reward?
   **e.** Did any event happen three times? Was there a special reason for this number?
   **f.** What was the importance of the magic object, the doll?
   **g.** Does this story give you any insights about the Russian people?

The characteristics can be posted in the room, or individual copies given the children, so that they can refer to them while finding these elements in stories they read on their own.

Familiar fairy tales as well as less common tales should be available in the classroom. A wide variety makes it possible for children to select a tale at their own reading level and to fulfill their need for either familiarity or challenge. The children's independent reading should be followed by a sharing time during which they discuss what they read and how their stories fit the fairy tale characteristics. This naturally leads to making relevant comparisons.

## Animal Tales

Animal tales include three subcategories: trickster stories, fables, and pourquoi tales. Refer to Chapter 1 for a more complete explanation of the tale characteristics.

Trickster, or beast, stories contain one central character, usually a trickster in animal shape, who is both a hero and a scoundrel. Trickster stories include *The Ox of the Wonderful Horns* by Ashley Bryan, *Anansi the Spider* by Gerald McDermott, *Tales of Uncle Remus* by Julius Lester, and *The Naked Bear* by John Bierhorst.

A fable is an animal story with a specific lesson, generally stated at the beginning or end. Examples include collections of fables by Aesop and *Jataka Tales* by Nancy DeRoin. Individual fables are retold in picture books such as *Once a Mouse* by Marcia Brown and *The Town Mouse and the Country Mouse* by Janet Stevens.

Pourquoi tales explain specific phenomena dealing with animals, such as why the bear lost his tail or why the leopard has spots. Typical stories include *Why Mosquitos Buzz in People's Ears* by Verna Aardema and *How Many Spots Does a Leopard Have?* by Julius Lester.

**LESSON OBJECTIVE:**  To introduce animal stories and classify the three types of tales.

**MATERIALS:**  Any of the stories mentioned above.

**PROCEDURE:**  The same format can be used with animal tales as was used with fairy tales. The number of lessons this will require depends on the grade level and prior knowledge of the group.

1. Read a story from each kind of animal tale for enjoyment.
2. State the characteristics of animal tales:
   a. Main characters are animals who act like people.
   b. The stories teach about life, usually lessons concerning personal traits and getting along with others.

3. Guide the children in noting the differences among trickster tales, fables, and pourquoi tales.
4. Ask the children to find the characteristics in the model tale. During the oral discussion, pupils can simultaneously write their ideas and ideas of others in their journals or jotting books.
5. Have the children read individual tales, noting the similarity and differences from the model tales. They can add to the notes they have written during the group lesson by applying those characteristics to the story they are now reading.
6. Have the children share their experiences of reading individual stories by
   a. Writing the title of their tale on a classroom chart of the three types of animal tales
   b. Reporting to the class or to their small group with reasons that their tale fits in that particular category, using notes they have written as a basis for their conclusions

## Legends and Myths

The difference between legends and myths is not easy to discern. The teacher can use either the direct format of the lessons described above and teach legends and myths separately, or teach by comparing the myth and the legend. With some groups, modeling each category separately, and then comparing (before the children are asked to attempt categorizing on their own) is most effective. The Venn diagram in Figure 4.1 offers a visual comparison of the similarities and differences between legends and myths, as explained in Chapter 1. The following representative legends can be used for modeling: *The Hallowed Horse* by Demi, *Tikki Tikki Tembo* by Arlene Mosel, *Buffalo Woman* by Paul Goble, and *The Chinese Mirror* by Mirra Ginsburg. Representative myths to use for modeling are as follows: *In the Beginning* by Virginia Hamilton, *The Summer Maker, Ojibway Indian Myth* by Margery Bernstein and Janet Kobrin, *Arrow to the Sun* by Gerald McDermott, and *A God on Every Mountain Top* by Byrd Baylor.

## MAKING RELEVANT COMPARISONS

In studying folk literature, the comparing and contrasting of stories develop almost spontaneously. In a sixth-grade class, when

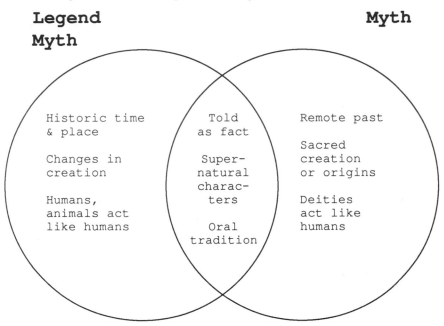

FIGURE 4.1    Venn diagram comparing myths and legends.

"Vassilissa the Fair" was being read, children interrupted the story to exclaim, "That's like 'Cinderella!'" Refining this ability can take many avenues:

1. Compare folktales from the same country for use of figurative language typical of that culture, recurring characters, and story structure.
2. Compare folktales from different countries and note the differences in the three elements stated above.
3. Compare universal themes and character traits shared by many cultures.
4. Compare the similarity and difference in what makes people laugh or enjoy the stories.

The three sample lessons presented here are designed to develop the students' ability to compare relevant information from multiple sources and recognize agreement or contradiction.

## Comparing Myths with Similar Themes

LESSON OBJECTIVE:  To compare two myths with similar themes and common motifs and be able to recognize similarities and differences.

MATERIAL:  An African myth *A Story, A Story* by Gail Haley; a Native American story of the Seneca tribe from *Keepers of the Earth* by Michael Caduto and Joseph Bruchac, page 3; journals or jotting books.

PROCEDURE:

1. Ask the children where they think the stories come from. Brainstorm and record ideas in journals.
2. Introduce the two accounts of how stories began, stating that you will compare these accounts with their findings. Direct the pupils to draw a vertical line down the middle of the next page of their notebook. To the left of the line, write "*A Story, A Story,* African myth," and to the right, "Native American Seneca myth."
3. Read *A Story, A Story* using a directed listening–thinking approach, stopping periodically to ask:
   a. What do you think will happen next?
   b. Why do you think so?
   c. (Later in story) Did it happen the way you expected? If not, what changed and why?
4. Read the Seneca Indian story from *Keepers of the Earth* (page 3) following the same procedure.
5. Guide the discussion by asking questions related to the elements of a story, such as
   a. What is the same about the setting? the characters? the problem? how the actions unfold? the resolution? (Ask each separately.)
   b. What is different about the setting? characters? problem? actions? resolution?
      *Note:* Children are able to respond to similarities more quickly than to differences. When adapting this lesson with appropriate stories for young children, the teacher must be very sure to elicit similarities first, and then ask probing questions to build recognition of differences.
   c. Which were more important, the things that were alike or the things that were different in the two stories?

**6.** Now compare together the legends and the ideas expressed in the brainstorming at the beginning of the lesson. Be sure that the pupils realize that the myths were told long before people went to school. Were these accounts really believed? If so, why?

## Comparing Variants of the Same Tale

The fact that the same tale appears in the folk literature of many different countries, with variations that usually result from cultural differences, is intriguing to both the young and the adult reader. Developing the ability to compare these variations can lead to interest in finding out more about different countries and peoples both geographically and culturally. Currently, the best source of variants with extensive cross-indexing is *The Storyteller's Sourcebook* by Margaret Read MacDonald (1982). Variant tales from Native American tribes are listed in *The Mythology of North America* by John Bierhorst (1985). One can select a favorite tale and find the source of variants, or trace a motif and find the tales from different countries that share that motif.

Comparison charts offer a visual means of organizing the similarities and differences children find in stories. Charts can be an individual or group project. The teacher or children select their own criteria for comparison, such as fairy, animal, legend, or myth characteristics or questions about the content. The chart in Figure 4.2 was made by a fifth-grader who enjoyed reading as many "Cinderella" stories as she could find. She chose her own questions and completed the chart as an independent project. The chart lists, along the side, five "Cinderella" titles and the retellers. Across the top, Dulci chose to compare: What country is the story from? What is the name of the main character? What kind of magic turns Cinderella into someone beautiful? How does the prince test women to find Cinderella? What happened to the stepsisters?

A similar chart can become a whole-class project, with the class choosing points of comparison and each child adding information from a different version.

The following lesson offers a way to compare two, rather than several, variants of the same type of tale. Figure 4.3 shows a chart made by Mrs. Afendoulis's third-graders to compare the tales they read.

**FIGURE 4.2**  Dulci explains her chart comparing Cinderella tales from many countries.

**LESSON OBJECTIVE:**   To note likeness and difference between two variants of similar "Cinderella" versions and produce the results on a Venn diagram.

**MATERIALS:**   *Cinderella* (German) retold by the Brothers Grimm, illustrated by Nonny Hogrogian; *Cinderella* (French) by Charles Perrault, translated and illustrated by Diane Goode (1988); 12-by-18 sheets of manila paper; large chart paper for teacher's model.

**PROCEDURE:**

1. Read the two "Cinderella" stories to the class, preferably at different sittings. Before reading each story, locate the country of origin on the globe. Observe that they are neighbors and ask the class to predict whether their stories will be more alike than different.
2. When reading the second tale, ask the children to think about how this story is like or different from the other story. Stop occasionally for comments, but be sure to maintain the flow of the story.
3. Give a large manila paper to a group of two or three pupils who are sitting together. If you have given previous instruction on

## Cinderella Stories

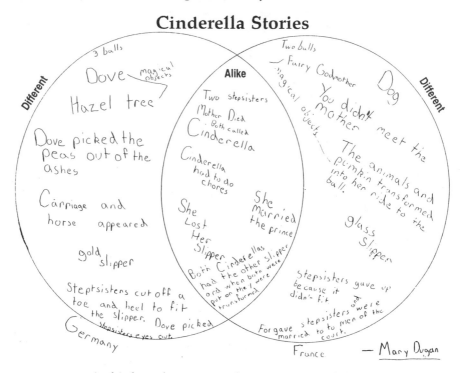

**FIGURE 4.3**  A third-grader compared two versions of Cinderella using a Venn diagram.

using Venn diagrams, you can ask them to make two overlapping circles. If this is a first encounter, model making the circles on your paper, telling the children that the overlapping part should be big enough to write in several phrases. Label the outer parts of the circle "different" and the inner part, "alike."

4. Begin by asking for a few similar, then different, items, all of which you write in the circles. Then encourage the children to continue on their own, having the books available for them to consult if needed.

5. End the lesson by sharing the items listed, recording the children's offerings on the large chart and asking the children to add to their own charts. The purpose of the lesson is to recognize as many areas of likeness and difference as possible, not to evaluate which children found the most.

After Mrs. Afendoulis presented this lesson to the Collins School third-graders, she reported that children were producing Venn diagrams in their reading journals, comparing other books they read throughout the fairy tale study. Lively sharing sessions led to exchange of books and more indepth reading.

## Comparing a Book and a Film

Some films are based directly on the written versions of the fairy tale or legend. The mental images the reader received from hearing or reading the book can be compared with the images of the film. For such a comparison, the book should be read first. Another comparison can direct attention to the degree of emotion. Did the students have the same or different feelings after reading the book and after viewing the film? A third type of comparison would be in understanding the story. What did the children understand better from the book? What did they understand better after seeing the film?

The following lesson plan is based on a film and book that were made from different sources of the same legend. Therefore the interpretations are quite different.

**LESSON OBJECTIVE:**  To compare a film and a book presentation of the same legend and evaluate the effectiveness of portrayal of character, setting, and similarities or differences in the plot.

**MATERIAL:**  *The Loon's Necklace,* book by William Toye and film by B. F. Sound Films (1981).

*Note:* The use of symbolism is developed much more extensively in the film than in the book, with the number 4 used in the medicine man's healing orders, in shooting arrows to the sky, and with the dives into the water. The shell necklace had meaning as part of the medicine man's tradition before it became the loon's necklace.

**PROCEDURE:**

1. Show the film. Note that the film was made before the book.
2. Read the book aloud to the class.
3. Guide a discussion developing the following points:
   a. How differently legends can be interpreted by different storytellers

**b.** The character of the old man as revealed in each medium
**c.** The differences between the stories
   Which story was more exciting?
   Which let you sense what was going to happen next more
   clearly?
   Which included more detail?
   Compare the illustrations in the book with the film.
**4.** Provide for creative response. The dramatic quality of this legend and the use of authentic masks in the film lead quite naturally into mask-making and dramatic role-playing.


## MAKING JUDGMENTS

   The extent to which the teacher is able to develop this skill will
be determined by the developmental level of the child. Social interaction is important so that the readers can realize that others have
similar or different interpretations of the same story. They learn to
value their own opinions and the opinions of others. Developing this
ability helps readers progress beyond making such statements as "I
liked it," "It was sad," and "It was funny," to provide reasons for
their opinions about the stories.
   Three lessons are described here. The teaching strategy for each
basically follows a sequence of teacher guidance: state the purpose of
the lesson, read the story or show the film, guide a discussion during
and after reading or showing, and provide for pupil response
throughout the experience.

### Judgments Concerning Interpretation of a Story

LESSON OBJECTIVE:   To lead to new understandings of characters
and/or culture as revealed by the story.
MATERIAL:   "The Girl Who Was Already Queen," from *Tales from
the Roof of the World* by Gioia Timpanelli; journals or notebooks.
PROCEDURE:
**1.** Show the group where Tibet is on the globe and share some information from the introduction of the book concerning Tibet
and the beliefs of the followers of Buddha. Knowledge of the term

*karma* is needed to understand the story. Karma is the Buddhist belief that the totality of a person's actions in the successive states of existence determines his or her fate in the next state of existence, i.e., his or her destiny.

2. State that the purpose of reading this story is to learn to understand about people by thinking about what you read.

3. Stop after reading about how the family's fortune changes. Ask the students if they agree with the reason the father gives for their good fortune?

4. Stop again after the girl is driven from home. Keep the questioning open-ended so that the answers are not what the listeners think you want but what they really are thinking. Simply ask what they think now and why.

5. At the third stopping place state that when you ask questions everyone does not get to answer. Now everyone may write in their journals their thoughts about how the girl escaped the bandits.

6. Finish the story. Ask the group to write about the meaning of the title, why was she already a queen.

7. Provide time for the class to share their writings in small groups and to discuss why they wrote what they did. This helps the child who had few ideas learn from the others.

With repetition and variations of this kind of thinking about stories, responses from the children become increasingly thoughtful. Expressing thoughts in talking and writing generates clearer thinking. The Russian "Baba Yaga" stories work well with this strategy.

## Analyzing and Evaluating Conclusions

**LESSON OBJECTIVE:** To be able to analyze and evaluate conclusions drawn in a story.

**MATERIAL:** Animal stories are appropriate for introducing this critical reading skill. The behavior of the trickster is clearly stated and easier to analyze than more complex tales. Select stories from collections such as *How Many Spots Does a Leopard Have?* by Julius Lester or *Favorite Folktales from Around the World* by Jane Yolen.

**PROCEDURE:**
1. Read the story to the class.
2. Discuss three questions:
    **a.** How does the storyteller present the character convincingly?
    **b.** What can you learn about the culture of the people who told this tale?
    **c.** What lessons did the people want to teach in this story?
3. After children have read animal stories on their own, ask them to answer the above questions from their independent reading. Vary the mode of response: oral discussion, making a comparison chart, informal thought writing, or writing an essay.

## Appreciating Illustrated Books

Currently, numerous versions of single folktales are being published with profuse and brilliant artwork. The art of the picture book is valuable not only for enhancing the text but also for exposing children to a variety of art styles. While working with a number of sixth-grade classes, I found that many children tend to pay little attention to the illustrations, but after making comparisons, they became interested in and skilled at comparing and evaluating the artist's contribution to the story.

**LESSON OBJECTIVE:**   To make judgments about the contribution of illustration to understanding, sensing, and appreciating the story.
**MATERIAL:**  See list below for examples of books from specific countries.
**PROCEDURE:**  Before implementing the plan, decide how much of the following will be teacher-directed discussion, when to move into small groups, and what written response will be encouraged. Some of the questions could be reproduced for the small groups to consider.
1. Discuss your objective in looking at the pictures in several illustrated folktales from one country.
2. Define terms that students will need to know, such as *artist's style*. The concept should include the way the artist interprets the story as shown by choice of medium, color, and the use of line.
3. Focus on one or more of the following to help the students analyze the artwork:

a. What does the picture tell you (content)?

b. How much of the story can you imagine by looking at the picture? What does the artist use to get you to imagine?

c. Does the artist's style fit the story? Why or why not?

d. Why do you think the artist chose that medium for the book?

e. Describe the colors each artist uses.

f. Describe how the lines of the drawings are similar or different.

g. (If mood has been explained) What kind of a feeling do you get about the mood of the story from each artist?

Comparing different artists' interpretation of folktales from one country helps children recognize that different approaches are valid and that everyone does not receive the same visual images. The following books are recommended for comparison:

**AFRICA**
*Mufaro's Beautiful Daughters* by John Steptoe
*Anansi the Spider* by Gerald McDermott
*Who's in Rabbit's House?* by Verna Aardema; illustrated by Leo and Diane Dillon
*A Story, A Story* by Gail Haley
*A Village of Round and Square Houses* by Ann Grifalconi

**NATIVE AMERICAN**
*Her Seven Brothers* by Paul Goble (and others by him)
*Arrow to the Sun* by Gerald McDermott
*Dancing Teepees* by Virginia Driving Hawk Sneve; illustrated by Stephen Gammell
*The Fire Bringer* by Margaret Hodges; illustrated by Peter Parnall
*A God on Every Mountain Top* by Byrd Baylor; illustrated by Carol Brown

**MEXICAN AND CENTRAL AMERICAN**
*The Riddle of the Drum* by Verna Aardema; illustrated by Tony Chen
*The Lady of Guadaloupe* by Tomie dePaola
*Spirit Child* by John Bierhorst; illustrated by Barbara Cooney
*Why the Corn Is Golden* by Vivien Blackmore; illustrated by Susana Martinez-Ostos
*Arroz con leche* by Lulu Delacre

**CHINESE**
*Liang and the Magic Paintbrush* by Demi
*Tikki Tikki Tembo* by Arlene Mosel; illustrated by Blair Lent
*Six Chinese Brothers* by Chieng Hou-tien
*Yeh-Shen* by Ai-Ling Louie; illustrated by Ed Young
*Suho and the White Horse* by Yuzo Otsuka; illustrated by Suekichi
   Akaba

**RUSSIAN**
*Baba Yaga* by Ernest Small; illustrated by Blair Lent
*Babushka* by Charles Mikolaycak
*Anna and the Seven Swans* by Maida Silverman; illustrated by David
   Small
*The Fool of the World and the Flying Ship* by Arthur Ransome; illus-
   trated by Uri Shuleviz
*Mazel and Shlimazel* by Isaac Bashevis Singer; illustrated by Margot
   Zemach

## RECOGNIZING THEMES

Along with the themes of the folktales come the moral and ethi-
cal values that are inherent in the stories as a part of the culture of
the people. The storyteller uses certain concepts, images, and sen-
suous experiences that bring to life the people, action, and scene in
the stories. The readers bring their own beliefs, personality, past experiences, associations, and mood of the moment to their contem-
plation of the stories. This produces a unique experience for each
reader. The role of the teacher is to foster a relationship between the
story and the reader that focuses on the literary work. The teacher
cannot ignore the particular bias of the story, or his or her own eth-
ical bias, but must assist the readers in understanding their own
moral values through reading the story. Three lessons are directed
toward helping children probe the meaning of stories they read.

### Recognizing the Same Theme in Different Stories

**LESSON OBJECTIVE:**   To recognize the same theme developed in different stories from different points of view.

MATERIAL: *The Lazies: Tales of the People of Russia* told by Mirra Ginsburg.

PROCEDURE:

1. Describe theme as a message from the author that tells us something about life. The book *The Lazies* is a collection of stories passed down from family to family in Russia to warn people about bad habits.
2. Ask prereading questions:
   a. What bad habit do you think is the theme of these stories?
   b. How do you think the author will warn you about laziness?
3. Read two stories: "Lazy Shedula" and "The Princess Who Learned to Work." After each story, elicit responses on how the author revealed the theme.
   a. How did the author show you that Shedula was lazy? that the princess was lazy?
   b. What did the characters do and say that show the results of laziness?
4. Compare the way the storyteller gives the message in each tale.
   a. How does "The Princess Who Learned to Work" warn against laziness?
   b. How is the way this story warns different from the message in "Lazy Shedula?"
   c. Can you say in your own words what the theme of each story is?

## Understanding Themes in Fables

A fable is a complex tale. Even though it is short and concise, many young readers cannot understand how the stated moral or proverb relates to the episodes of the story. Through oral sharing of a number of Aesop's fables, the teacher can direct the students to recognize those elements of the story that point to the moral stated.

Nancy Oosterink, a third-grade teacher at Sandy Hill Elementary School in Jenison, Michigan, guided her class to understand fable themes through storytelling by using story line illustrations. She introduced fables by telling a personal story about how she planned to spend all her earnings from her childhood job and found that she had earned much less than she expected. They talked about the lesson that she had learned, and she told them this was a common habit, and someone had written a fable about it. Then she read Aesop's "The Country Maid and the Milk Pail," telling the moral before reading the story. Half-way through the story the children predicted what would happen, and afterwards they discussed how the moral could be illustrated in the fable.

They retold the story together and discussed what they would draw if they wanted to use illustrations at the beginning, middle, and end. Mrs. Oosterink modeled the procedure by drawing on an overhead transparency that had the title and the moral of the fable printed at the top. Following their advice, she drew a picture in colored marker for the beginning, the middle, and the end of the fable.

The children worked together in groups of three. Each group was given copies of a different fable from Michael Hague's version of *Aesop's Fables*. Each group read the fable together, and each member of the group was responsible for illustrating either the beginning, the middle, or the end of the tale, and sharing orally that part of the fable with the class. Each child drew on a third of a transparency with colored markers. The beginning, middle, and end illustrations were taped together and the title and moral of the fable written on the sheet. After the illustrations were completed, they practiced retelling the story together. Each group told the fable to the class, projecting their illustrations for all to see. They were prepared to explain how their illustrations fit the moral of the story if they should be asked by the listeners.

### Recognizing Unstated Themes

Even though the moral is stated, the relationship between the story action and the moral is implied, not stated. Therefore oral discussion is necessary to help the readers see how they are making inferences.

LESSON OBJECTIVE:   To use the skill gained from finding story elements in fables to discover unstated themes in other stories.
MATERIAL:   A folktale with a clear but unstated theme, such as *The Third Gift* by Jan Carew, *Liang and the Magic Paintbrush* by Demi, or *Ladder to the Sky* by Barbara Esbensen.

**PROCEDURE:** Teacher guidance will help develop the questioning attitude that leads to thinking beyond the plot to the message the storyteller wishes to share.

1. State that in reading this story we want to discover the message the story tells about life.
2. Ask questions during and after the reading, such as:
   **a.** What is the purpose of the character's actions?
   **b.** What happens in the story that gives you clues as to what the author wants to tell the reader?
   **c.** Can you find a conversation that gives a clue? How does that help you decide what the message is?

### SUMMARY

Thinking critically while reading is a conscious effort. Therefore be sure to state the objective of your lesson to the group you are teaching. At the end of the lesson, ask them to reiterate what you were teaching. The objectives of the specific critical reading lessons in this chapter are to classify types and characteristics of folktales, to draw comparisons, to make judgments based on text and artwork, and to recognize themes.

Informal writing as a means of expressing thoughts about the story generates a freedom to use writing as self-expression and a concrete experience for putting thoughts into words. The evaluation of student writing should be done only for determining what aspect of the teaching needs to be clarified and what writing strategies need to be taught.

The strategies used with these four skills can be adapted for any other aspect of critical reading and for other genres of literature. Sixth-graders who had scored low in a critical reading test made significant gains after three months of instruction based on these procedures (Bosma, 1981).

If this sounds like heavy fare for your children, begin with comparing two humorous stories just for fun. For the intermediate grades I recommend "The Professor of Smells" from *The Rainbow People* by Laurence Yep and "The Unwilling Magician" from *Tales from the Roof of the World* by Gioia Timpanelli. For primary children, choose *Tikki Tikki Tembo* retold by Arlene Mosel and *Turtle Knows Your Name* by Ashley Bryan.

Whenever folk literature is used to improve the art and skill of reading, it is important to maintain enjoyment of the stories. The strategies explained in this chapter are intended to advance interest in and appreciation of the literature, rather than provide a minute examination of the details, which lessens children's interest in reading.

# 5

# Learning to Write
# with Folk Literature

The purpose of writing down the stories was to pass them on to a
larger audience than could be reached by storytelling and to keep the
stories from being lost to ensuing generations. The goal of teaching
writing in the elementary classroom is to develop children's ability
to communicate through their own writing, to teach them to appreciate writing, and to make them better readers. The study of folk
literature fosters the reading–writing connection. For example, a
fourth-grade social studies unit on the southwestern United States at
the Grand Haven, Michigan, Christian School included listening to
and reading many Native American tales. One pupil was particularly
intrigued, and she read and reread the legends. During writing time
one day she shared with her teacher a poem she was writing, ob-
viously influenced by her reading of Native American tales:

> One day a boy asked his Grandfather,
> "What are Indian colors?"
> They are green grass, blue sky, red dirt,
> yellow sun, orange clay,
> brown, white, grey, and black horses,
> silver scales of fish.
> Boy, do not forget these colors!
> Some day they might be gone with the wind,
> Just a memory! Just a memory!
> *Wendy DeWitt*

In Chapter 4 writing was discussed as a tool for learning. This chapter provides ideas for teaching writing by using folk literature as a model of form, theme, and content. Figure 5.1 offers a visual form of the writing models.

## FOLKTALE FORM

The predictable structure of the folktale, which assists the reader in understanding the story, also serves to help the writer formulate a story. Many of the nursery tales contain a recurring phrase or rhyme, which the reader can anticipate by the rhythm of the story. In "The Three Little Pigs," the young listener quickly joins in on "He huffed, and he puffed" and in "The Three Billy Goats Gruff" expects to hear "trip, trap" when each billy goat goes over the bridge.

Other stories, such as "The House That Jack Built," are written with cumulative patterns in which each episode is built upon the previous one with a predictable overlapping structure.

Many fairy tales share beginning phrases such as "Once upon a time," immediately introduce the characters, and tell the story in a direct manner with the ending firmly stated. This matches the child's narrative sense and can be used to encourage the reluctant writer.

For children at any grade level, prewriting activities provide a helpful way to begin. Prewriting provides the action and participation needed to stimulate creation. Providing them with story starters is not enough for many writers. They need practice with words and ideas before they feel comfortable writing on their own.

### Repetitive Story Patterns

*The Great Big Enormous Turnip* by Alexei Tolstoy, or a similar book with repetitive phrases, is a good beginning to use in a prewriting activity. First read the story, with the children chanting the repetitive phrase. Then display sentence strips prepared with names or a key word omitted. Elicit original names or words to produce a variant of the story. This can begin as a group activity and become individual storymaking as soon as the child is ready.

Group story writing helps the reluctant writer. It is easier to provide a word or phrase than to create an entire idea. Confidence builds as the child sees the writing process happening. Listening to other

FIGURE 5.1.   A web of ways to use folktales as models for writing.

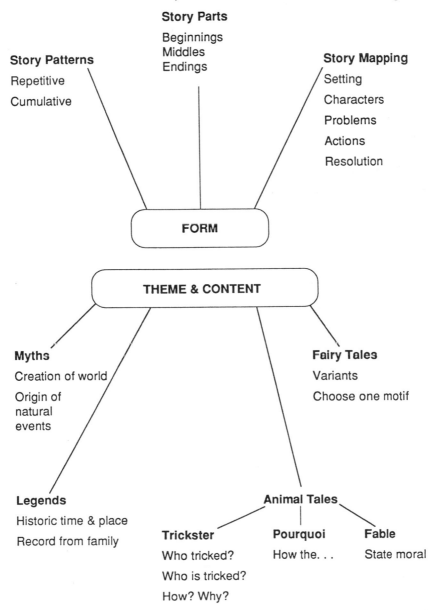

**Story Parts**
Beginnings
Middles
Endings

**Story Patterns**
Repetitive
Cumulative

**Story Mapping**
Setting
Characters
Problems
Actions
Resolution

FORM

THEME & CONTENT

**Myths**
Creation of world
Origin of
natural
events

**Fairy Tales**
Variants
Choose one motif

**Legends**
Historic time & place
Record from family

**Animal Tales**

**Trickster**
Who tricked?
Who is tricked?
How? Why?

**Pourquoi**
How the. . .

**Fable**
State moral

children's ideas stimulates participation. After children listen and respond orally to familiar stories such as Paul Galdone's versions of *Billy Goats Gruff, Henny-Penny,* or *The Gingerbread Boy,* they can create a new story. When the group responds to oral creating, the teacher records the process on chart paper.

**LESSON OBJECTIVE:**  To build a new story using the form of a familiar tale.

**MATERIALS:**  Lesson is based on *Billy Goats Gruff,* as an example; you may choose another story if you prefer.

**PROCEDURE:**

1. Discuss the components of the story. How many billy goats are there? Where did they go? How did they get there? What is the problem? What words do you hear repeated? Fill out a chart like the one below with the children's responses.

2. Plan the main components of the new story in comparison to the story read. Ask for ideas for animals, places to go, how to get there, the danger along the way, and the repetitive phrase or question. The process chart below was made with first-graders.

| FOLKTALE | OUR STORY |
| --- | --- |
| Three billy goats | Three teddy bears |
| To the meadow | To the berry patch |
| Across the bridge | Through the forest |
| An ugly troll | A giant who eats bears |
| Trip, trap | Thud, thump |
| Who's going over my bridge? | Who's going across my path? |

3. Next brainstorm a descriptive word chart. What words were used in the folktale that told us about the characters? What words should we use for our story?

| FOLKTALE | OUR STORY |
| --- | --- |
| *Billy goats:* | *Teddy bears:* |
| Youngest | Littlest |
| Tiniest | Middle-sized |
| Second | Great big |
| Bigger | First |
| Third | Second |
| Biggest | Third |

*Troll:*             *Giant:*
   Ugly              Wicked
   Mean            Enormous

4. Begin group composing, with the process chart and the word chart taped alongside a fresh piece of chart paper. Record when a consensus is reached about the content. This may take longer than one period. Review the process and word chart if the lesson continues to a second setting to provide the continuity that is needed to create the end product.

How similar the new story and the folktale are will depend on the creative freedom of the group. Some children need to hold onto the familiar structure throughout many experiences, and others are ready to move freely to a new creation. This lesson format can be used with older children having difficulty with writing. Read interesting, simple stories such as *Wiley and the Hairy Man* by Molly Bang or *Strega Nona* by Tomie dePaola.

## Cumulative Tales

The same procedure used with the nursery tales can be used with cumulative tales, using charts for planning. The writing lesson should be preceded by the sharing of several books with predictable patterns such as *Henny-Penny* by Paul Galdone, *One Fine Day* by Nonny Hogrogian, *Bringing the Rain to Kapiti Plain* by Verna Aardema, and *The Fisherman and His Wife* by the Grimms. *It Could Always Be Worse* by Margot Zemach, and *Tikki Tikki Tembo* by Arlene Mosel offer more sophisticated patterns; they can be used after the children have enjoyed and recognized the patterns in simpler tales. The following lesson format could be based on any one of the cumulative tales.

**LESSON OBJECTIVE:** To guide the children in sentence building by adding adjectives or changing verbs. (Begin with selecting one or the other; do not do both in one lesson)
**MATERIAL:** *One Fine Day* retold by Nonny Hogrogian; chart paper; figures from the story, traced and cut from tagboard (optional).
**PROCEDURE:**
1. Reread the story, using the figures to trigger the pupils' memory of story sequence.

2. Note that the storyteller was eager to tell us what would happen next and did not use many words to describe the characters or objects in the story.
3. Select phrases or sentences from the story that contain one adjective or none. Guide the children to add other words to describe the fox, the cow, or the old woman.
4. After many words have been brainstormed, rewrite the last cumulative sequence, including a descriptive word provided by the children wherever one would fit.
5. When substituting verbs, consider dividing the long sentences into phrases so that the learners can sense the structure:

> Give me your jug / so I can fetch some water / to give the field / to get some grass / to feed the cow . . .

A second-grader at Stepping Stones Montessori School in Grand Rapids, Michigan, made these changes:

> A chestnut colored fox came upon a kind, wonderful miller and asked him, "Oh please, kind miller, give me a little grain to give to the chuckling, big, fat hen to get a hard-boiled white egg . . ."

## Using Fairy Tales to Begin the Story

The narrative form of the fairy tale provides a no-nonsense approach that helps the writer put thoughts down in a straightforward manner. This matches the oral story form that children have been using since learning to talk. When children begin to write, many have difficulty beginning or ending a story, or providing coherent action involving their chosen characters. Prewriting lessons, directed toward one of these elements, helps the young writer create.

Using the fairy tale story form does not limit the child to writing fairy tales. This form can be used for any content. The emphasis of prewriting lessons is not on what the child writes, but on how the child expresses the message in an interesting and complete style. Once children are comfortable with a direct narrative style, they will be able to depart from it and provide their own variations.

LESSON OBJECTIVE:   To help writers who have difficulty beginning their stories.
MATERIAL:   Fairy tales previously read to the class.

**PROCEDURE:**

1. Tell the group that you are going to think about the way the storytellers begin their stories.
2. Reread just the beginning phrases or first paragraph of fairy tales that were previously read to the class. Also read the beginnings of the same tale told by different authors. For example, *Cinderella* as told by the Grimms and by Perrault.
3. Ask the children which beginning makes them curious about what is going to happen and why. Ask which one tells them the most about the story.
4. Brainstorm a topic that the class could write about, but do not necessarily plan to create a story. This is a process lesson that will transfer to later writing. At this time, simply use the topics to create several beginnings.
5. Write the brainstormed beginnings on chart paper. Analyze each beginning with the class. Which one would make you want to read on? Why? Which one tells you what to expect in the story?
6. Since this is a process lesson that should transfer to later writing, end the lesson here. Later, when children are ready to write, remind them of this experience and encourage them to think of these models or look at a fairy tale for ideas.

## Ending the Story

A lesson on endings can follow a similar format, with a selection of endings from a variety of stories to analyze. Some cultures have distinctive endings for their tales. For example, Norwegian fairy tales often end with "Snip, snap, snout. This tale's told out."

Here are some steps you can take to help your students end their tales:

1. Ask children to read aloud the last paragraph or sentence from folktales that you have shared previously.
2. Discuss similarities and differences between examples.
3. Then brainstorm ending phrases and sentences. This process can help the writer avoid simply stopping and writing THE END.

## The Middle Section

Improving the middle section of the story requires a series of lessons in which children follow the sequence of the plot and examine how the storyteller develops the characters and action. The use of a story map helps organize the sequence of the main part of the story if it contains a problem. If the story form is repetitive, help the writer decide how many actions are needed to follow the pattern. For example, in *The Great Big Enormous Turnip* by Alexei Tolstoy, two people and three animals were called to help. Therefore, the middle of the story needed five episodes before the story can end.

Are the writers having trouble creating authentic characters? Look again at the folktales you have been reading together, and note the actions and conversations of the characters that help you understand their personalities. Generally, folktales contain few descriptions. The prewriting lesson described above in the "Cumulative Tales" section can help the children use descriptive words.

A story map is a practical planning device that helps the children think through their story ideas and provides a visual from which they can create. This is particularly helpful when time limits make it impossible to finish the story in one sitting. If the proposed story will present and solve a problem, reproduce the form shown in Figure 3.1. Vary the form to fit other story structures. In a third-grade class, children wrote independently using the form in Figure 5.2. Teachers who have used this procedure report that it has been a major factor in improving the quality of the writing of their pupils.

## FOLKTALE THEME AND CONTENT

Just as prewriting activities help writers understand story structure, informal writing helps writers capture ideas from the themes and content of the stories they hear. Informal writing is recorded in a journal or notebook that is kept by the child; it is neither evaluated nor edited by the teacher.

After the teacher reads a story aloud, many children are eager to make a remark about the story—about personal experiences, the artwork, some words that caught their fancy, or a reaction to the char-

CREATE YOUR OWN FAIRYTALE

| Who's in your story? | Where are they going? | How will they get there? |
|---|---|---|
| | | |
| Who will try to stop them? | What will he or she say as each one sees him? | Descriptive words. |
| | | |

FIGURE 5.2   A story structure chart helps children organize their original tales.

acters, action, or ending of the story. There is never time to listen to everyone. Following discussion, informal writing presents an opportunity to make the writing a continuation of the thinking process stimulated by the oral interchange. The critical reading lessons in Chapter 4 include informal writing as part of the thinking strategy. If the teacher develops the habit of providing a few moments for the children to write these thoughts down, they become more familiar with writing as a communication process and also recognize that their thoughts are important and worth recording. These recorded thoughts can become the stimulus for a poem or topic for a story at a later time.

## Myths

Origins are intriguing to children. Even the child who has difficulty recognizing and verbalizing imaginative thoughts can take a "what if" stance and provide fanciful explanations for how things came to be.

**LESSON OBJECTIVE:**  To create a myth.
**MATERIAL:**  *In the Beginning* by Virginia Hamilton.
**PROCEDURE:**
1. Read several myths from this collection. The most effective results will come if the writing lesson is planned along with critical reading. See the lesson comparing myths of similar theme in Chapter 4.
2. Lead children in brainstorming other ideas for explaining the origin of the phenomena in the myths that were read.
3. Choose a country, perhaps one that you are currently studying in social studies, to be the setting for the myth.
4. Discuss which people would be the audience for the story, in other words, which cultural group will be given an explanation for this happening.
5. Encourage the children to select from the brainstormed lists or use their own idea to write an explanation of how some natural phenomenon began in that particular country.

You may wish to limit the topic to one natural phenomenon. For example, *The Summer Maker* or *The First Morning* by Margory Bernstein and Janet Kobrin, or *How Summer Came to Canada* by William Toye both explain the origin of seasons. The writers can choose a season and provide their own explanations.

The brainstorming process is important for generating ideas. The more stories that the students hear, the better they become at producing their own writing. The sense of story, which is refined through hearing literary models, becomes the spring from which ideas flow.

After a lesson based on the above procedure, a fourth-grader at Rehoboth Christian School, Rehoboth, New Mexico, wrote the following myth:

A long time ago the Sun, Moon, and Stars all shone during the day. The people hated it because the farmers' crops withered, the windows melted from the hot sun, and all of the plants dried up. There was no water for the river, so the people couldn't have any water to drink, and the babies could not get to sleep.

So then the Sun, Moon, and Stars quarreled about who

would shine during the night and who would shine during the day. Finally the Sun beat down on the Moon and Stars and said, "If you don't let me shine during the day, I will beat on you so bad that you will never be able to shine again!" So the Moon and Stars said they would shine during the night, and the Sun quit beating on them. And so the Sun shone during the day and the Moon and Stars shone at night.

The people were very happy! They had lots of rain, the crops grew good, the windows were replaced, and the babies could finally get to sleep.

*Jeff Boyd*

## Legends

The recording of oral folklore is not limited to the professional storyteller. Groups who have moved to America have produced folklore collections that reveal much about their culture. For example, the Cambodian people who settled on the south side of Minneapolis told their stories during a language project at Our Saviour Lutheran Church. The stories were collected and typed under the direction of Charles Numrich of Theatre Unlimited.

Byrd Baylor, author of stories about the Southwest, collected legends from Arizona Indian children and wrote them exactly as the children remembered hearing them from their parents and grandparents. The stories are published in her book, *And It Is Still That Way*.

Nancy DeVries, reading teacher as Kennedy Mid School, Gallup, New Mexico, collected folk anecdotes from a summer remedial reading class. The Indian and Hispanic children, who were reading *Tiger Eyes* by Judy Blume, encountered the phrase "when the lizards run." They had heard their mothers and grandmothers use that saying frequently. The group decided to ask their families what the saying meant and write down what they were told. The children wrote and edited their stories on computers using the Bank Street Writer word-processing program (see Figure 5.3). They were so excited about their writing that on the last day of school they chose computer time to finish copying their stories, instead of having a party. The explanations they gave varied greatly. Note that some have written the anecdote exactly as reported and others have expanded it into a story.

**FIGURE 5.3**  Sixth-graders in Gallup, New Mexico, rewrite their legends
using a computer software program.

In the Navajo way, first my Grandpa told me every spring the
lizards run because, they have been under the ground for so
long. When winter comes they go underground for the winter.
After the winter they come out of the ground. Then they run
around in the summer.

*Vernon Yazzie*

When the lizards run is because the ancestors are coming back
to live in the spring. The ancestors used to race lizards for
money a long time ago, to see who runs the fastest. Some
ancestors used to sell them to the white men.

*Ross*

When the lizards run it is time for spring. It is time for joy and
laughter and spring showers. Spring showers wash down and
melt snow so lizards could run around freely. I like it when the

lizard run because I chase them all over the place. It is fun . . .
they cheer you up and make you laugh when you are sad or un-
happy.

                                                                    *Shawn*

I'll hear the birds singing. I'll smell the lilac bushes, and I'll
watch the iris bloom. Cuands los lagartijos corren . . . life is a
good adventure in the spring. Lizards wake us up to get us
ready for the fun of summer.

                                                                   *Miguel*

Nancy DeVries reported:

Remedial students, "sentenced" to summer school, developed
sophisticated skills in creating and revising during the writing
process, and were able, many for the first time, to have a real
pride of accomplishment in their work. An additional value that
developed from using folk literature was a sharing of cultural
stories and heritages, and with this sharing a mutual respect
emerged, rather than the previous aloof distrust prevalent between the different Indian tribes and Spanish or Anglo ethnic
groups.

                                    *(Personal communication, September 1985)*

At Christmas time, Ms. DeVries's class wrote family folktales to
give as gifts to younger brothers, sisters, or cousins. The tales were
read or performed in class. One Indian girl discovered that some of
her ancestors were from the Acoma tribe. She retold and illustrated
the following story of Young Hunter told to her by her Acoma
grandmother (see Figure 5.4).

### YOUNG HUNTER

This is a story of the Acoma Indians. It is about a boy
named Young Hunter who had a big head and how he saved a
girl.

Long ago there lived a boy named Young Hunter. He was a
very shy boy because he had such a big ugly head. One day the
Chief called all the boys together for a meeting. Young Hunter

**FIGURE 5.4**  Kimberlee shows the class the setting for her Acoma legend.

joined the meeting. The Chief was talking about a girl named
Pink Flower who had been taken away by the Giant who lived
sixty miles away. He told them who ever saved her could marry
her or a girl called Turquoise Girl. So he packed his clothes and
said good-bye to his grandmother and left. He met a rain god
on the way and kept him for protection. They got to a mesa and
the rain god said, "I have to leave you here. Go on. Here are
some herbs. Chew them as you walk. Spit them out when you
see danger."

So he went on. Then he heard the god's voice say, "Don't
kill the Giant!"

The next day he saw the girl. He whispered, "Come, we
must go before the giant wakes up!"

So he spit out some of the herbs and they flew to where he
had left the rain god and all of a sudden he heard the giant
scream and die.

The next day he returned to the village with Pink Flower.
Everybody cheered. Turquoise Girl came to help the Grand-

mother. She was taken into a room filled with soft buckskin and strings of turquoise beads. She was taken into a room all bare except for a mask. The mask of a young hunter. The grand-mother said, "Young Hunter has passed his test!" She called Young Hunter into the room and a handsome man whom she had never seen before stepped into the room. On the day the marriage was celebrated Turquoise Girl made loaves of bread and did household tasks for the man she loved.

*Kimberlee Evans*

Folklore can be collected by all children, not only those who belong to a distinctively different culture. The collector can begin on the playground. *Anna Banana: 101 Jump-Rope Rhymes* collected by Joanna Cole can serve as a model for recording rhymes. The children can add hand claps and footchants that are popular today. *Once Upon a Folktale,* edited by Gloria Blatt (in press), includes a detailed plan for engaging a class in folklore gathering. The fifth-grade class de-scribed in that account invited parents and other classmates to a "Celebration of Folklore" at the end of their study.

Recording family legends can be an exciting and challenging class project. Preparation would include discussing procedures for talking to family members and recording the interviews. Appropriate ques-tions should be formulated in class for the children to take to the person who may know the stories. If possible, the child can collect the information on a tape recorder and then transcribe the tape. If no tape recorder is available, the child should write down everything the adult says. Having listened to many folktales, the child will be able to include the literary conventions of the folktale when rewrit-ing the information from the adult.

Alvin Schwartz's many books can serve as models for collecting lore. Schwartz travels throughout the country collecting stories, rhymes, and common sayings from ordinary people. Each of his books is meticulously documented with notes, sources, and ac-knowledgments. His first book, *A Twister of Twists, A Tangle of Tongues* grew from his personal collection of tongue twisters. This began a career of collecting folklore on a variety of subjects. See A Guide to Recommended Folk Literature for Children for represent-ative titles of his collections.

Collecting folklore is different from recording oral history because it is limited to traditional beliefs, customs, and expressions that have been absorbed by a group of people. This group could be a family, a culture group, or people in a geographic region. Collecting and recording lore adds an interesting component to an oral history study or could be a separate unit of study.

## Animal Tales

Animal tales provide an entertaining model for writing. Sample lessons given here for writing trickster stories, pourquoi tales, and fables can be adjusted to match the level of your pupils' writing progress. Some children need only to read the tales, and they are ready to try their own. Others need much guidance and benefit greatly from charts and forms. A good place to begin is with trickster stories because their structure and directness makes them easier than fables to compose.

**LESSON OBJECTIVE:**   To write a trickster tale.
**MATERIAL:**  Such trickster tales as *The Naked Bear* by John Bierhorst, *Tales of Uncle Remus* by Julius Lester, *Anansi the Spider* by Gerald McDermott, *The Ox of the Wonderful Horns* by Ashley Bryan.
**PROCEDURE:**
1. Share the tales.
2. As a prewriting activity, chart the stories using a form such as one shown in Figure 5.5.
3. Discuss the role of the trickster as sometimes a hero, sometimes a naughty tricker.

**FIGURE 5.5**   A chart for planning a trickster tale.

| NAME OF STORY | WHO TRICKED? | WHO WAS TRICKED? | TRICK | RESULT |
|---------------|--------------|------------------|-------|--------|
|               |              |                  |       |        |

4. When children are ready to write their trickster tales, they can outline or put in charts the needed elements in the story. They decide whether their animal will be a hero or a naughty tricker.
5. Consider creating a class trickster. Each pupil can write an adventure for the chosen animal.

Pourquoi animal tales are usually titled "Why the [name of animal] has [a particular feature]." These are similar to legends, but they are exaggerated and humorous because they were not believed and were created strictly for entertainment.

Mollie Carnes, a second-grade teacher at Pinewood Elementary School in Jenison, Michigan, guided her class in writing pourquoi tales, using the skeleton form of *The Baby Leopard,* an African folktale retold by Linda and Clay Goss (1989). She introduced the folktale by showing the students the book cover and explaining the pourquoi folktale. They talked about storytelling, and then students listened to the tape of the story, published by Bantam Audio Publishing. Several children listened to the tape again during their lunch hour or when other work was finished.

Later, Mrs. Carnes reread the story and together they filled in the chart with the form of the tale (see Figure 5.6). Then they brain-

**FIGURE 5.6** A chart for planning a pourquoi tale.

| HOW THE | GOT ITS | |
|---|---|---|
| Setting | Who else warns him? | How does he try to get rid of it? |
| BEGINNING | MIDDLE | END |
| What is the warning given to your animal by his mother? | What happens? | Does he succeed? |

stormed names of animals and special features that they would like to write about. They chose one for a group story, and using the map as a guide, produced a model tale. After that, each child chose an animal for a story and wrote his or her plan on an individual story map form.

After writing a tale, each child edited it by reading it aloud to him- or herself. Then a friend read it. After final proofreading was checked by Mrs. Carnes, the children were ready to recopy and illustrate. Eight-year-old Kelly Rabe wrote and illustrated the following story:

### HOW THE KITTEN GOT ITS PURR

Once upon a time there lived a little kitten. She was a curious kitten. One day, the kitten said, "Can I go out to play, Mommy?"

"Yes, you may, but under one condition, Baby kitten, Baby kitten, please don't mess with motors."

"I am not afraid of motors. Meeeeow!" She walked out. Baby kitten saw a fixit shop.

"Oh Hi," said the fixit man.

"Hello, Fixit man. Can I go into your fixit shop?"

"Yes, you may but under one condition, Baby kitten, Baby kitten, please don't mess with motors."

"I am not afraid of motors. Meeeeow!" She walked in. She was playing. A motor started to jiggle and it fell right into baby kitten's throat!

"Meeow," said Baby kitten.

All of a sudden a different sound came out of her mouth. The fixit man came running.

"Oh no! I warned you, Baby kitten."

Baby kitten went home. She tried to talk. But all that came out was a big purrrrr. She tried to get rid of it. She tried to cough it up. But it didn't work. Her mother said, "That's what you get for disobeying."

And that's how the kitten got its purrrrrrrrrrrr.

Arnold Lobel's original *Fables* (1981) provides an excellent model for children who are writing fables. Comparing modern fables with versions of Aesop and Jataka fables will ease the transition from reading the stories to writing them. Since composing a fable requires a relatively high level of thinking ability, this writing experience will be more productive above the third-grade level. After reading and discussing many fables, select one of two variant strategies:

1a. Make a list of morals or proverbs, such as "don't count your chickens before they hatch." Each child can select one moral or proverb as the theme for an original fable.
1b. Make a list of human faults in a brainstorming session. Practice making an original proverb that cautions against that fault. Write the story that provides an explanation, ending with a moral.
2. Using either 1a or 1b, elicit from the children possible characters and adjectives to describe them.

**Fairy Tales**

A comparison of a modern fairy tale, such as Jane Yolen's *The Girl Who Cried Flowers* (1974) or Oscar Wilde's *The Selfish Giant* (1968), and the traditional fairy tale demonstrates to children that writing fairy tales is a legitimate use of story form. This offers a good opportunity to discuss the difference between traditional stories and those originating from a known author. Direct pupils to check how the author is identified. Do they find the words *retold by, translated, compiled,* or similar expression? Are there notes concerning the origins of the stories? If not, the stories are modern, invented tales such as the ones children write. The comparison will also reveal that the modern fairy tale can be written more simply than the traditional tale, which usually interweaves many motifs.

The idea of selecting one motif as the topic of an original fairy tale helps develop the creative flow of ideas for the child writer.

LESSON OBJECTIVE: To write a fairy tale.
MATERIAL: A modern fairy tale such as Oscar Wilde's *The Selfish Giant* (1968) or Moira Miller, *In Search of Spring* (1988).
PROCEDURE:
1. Explain that this modern tale is original, rather than retold or written down from oral tradition. Review the characteristics of a fairy tale presented in Chapter 1. Read the story.

**2.** Compare this story with a familiar traditional fairy tale. Note the characteristics used in the modern tale.
**3.** To give the writer courage to attempt this more complicated story form, direct writers to choose one motif, such as three wishes, a seemingly impossible task, or a supernatural object, as a source of magic. A brainstorming session would be helpful in generating options for this choice.
**4.** After selecting the motif, encourage children to create the characters and setting for the story.
**5.** Encourage independent writing, and the sharing of stories with partners for help in preparing a final draft.

Guard against requiring the children to restage traditional tales in modern-day settings. These attempts are usually not successful below the age of twelve because time and space relationships are difficult for children to manipulate.

Students may write variants of familiar tales such as "Cinderella," "Snow White," or "Hansel and Gretel." To help them do this:

1. Begin by reading several different versions of the stories.
2. Discuss the similarities and differences.
3. Encourage the children to either create their own version or invent new characters and episodes following the story line of the modeled fairy tale.

Some children may elect to change the setting from the olden days to modern time, and such a choice would indicate that those children had developed a flexible sense of time and space.

### SUMMARY

In this chapter, writing is presented as an extension of oral language, with writing activities preceded by literature sharing. Basing lessons on the predictable folktale story form found in nursery stories, cumulative tales, and fairy tales helps the child write with confidence. The examples given in this chapter can be adjusted to any grade level, using other titles described in A Guide to Recommended

Folk Literature for Children or similar tales available in local libraries.

Involving children in collecting folklore promotes an awareness of how culture develops, a recognition of their own contribution to culture, and an appreciation for the culture of others. Recording folklore offers a real purpose for writing that can be shared with others.

Informal writing becomes a natural response to hearing, reading, and discussing literature. After providing for informal writing time, teachers can work with ideas recorded by the children by turning once again to folk literature for models to improve the writers' craft.

The content of folk literature offers a wealth of ideas for story making. Lessons using myths, legends, animal tales, and fairy tales provide opportunities for young writers to grow in their writing performance.

# 6

# Creative Activities with Folk Literature

The imaginative quality of folk literature clamors for creative response. Creative activities play an important role in developing understanding and appreciation of the stories and contribute a real purpose for the reading. This chapter contains suggestions for relating folktales to specific creative encounters. These ideas are presented with the assumption that creative drama, music, and art are already part of the school curriculum. Folktales can be the content of processes already practiced and enjoyed in the classrooms.

## IMPROVISING, PANTOMIMING, DRAMATIZING

After the introductions to fairy tales, animal stories, legends, and myths, children can share the stories they have read individually or in small groups by using creative movement. Expressive body movements reveal ideas and feelings that children receive from the story.

While drawing comparisons between two or more variants of tales, the similarities or differences can be shown by action. Dramatizing "The Gingerbread Boy" or "The Little Red Hen" is not only an enjoyable activity but shows the teacher that the children have understood the differences between the two tales.

Tomie dePaola's art and writing style make his versions of folk stories natural selections for play-acting. His illustrations are drawn from the perspective of an audience viewing a performance. *Strega Nona, The Lady of Guadaloupe,* or *The Clown of God* provide models for stage props and costumes for in-class performances. Nancy Willard's retelling of *East of the Sun and West of the Moon* is an excellent play script for older children.

A performance by a professional drama troupe or a nearby college group can be a catalyst for freeing children to participate in creative drama (see Figure 6.1).

Since fables generally have two or three main characters, pupils can develop a partner or team pantomime of the story, with little or no teacher direction. After the children have practiced, the rest of the class becomes the audience. If a narrator for each team states the moral of the fable, the audience will be able to follow the action of

**FIGURE 6.1**
A visiting drama troupe, United Stage Players, Grand Rapids, Michigan.

the pantomime and interpret the presentation. The use of simple masks enhances the fable presentation.

For ideas on implementing dramatic activities, see *Creative Drama in the Classroom* (McCaslin, 1984), *Improvisation Handbook* (Elkind, 1975), and *Informal Drama in the Elementary Language Arts Program* (Stewig, 1983). A book for the children to read to learn more about theater and get their own ideas for dramatization is *Theater Magic* (Bellville, 1986). She brings the reader right into the theater with the invitation, "When you leave the familiar world outside and enter a dimly lit theater, you can let your imagination go and become part of a story from any time and place" (p. 6).

## MASK MAKING

Children become less inhibited doing pantomime and improvisations when using masks. The mask does not hide the child but rather releases and reveals the child's ability to forget him- or herself and enter into the character.

The making of the mask can be simple: Cut card stock or tagboard into oval forms, with eyes and nose cut out, and yarn attached to tie around the child's head. A few simple felt-tip lines can designate eyebrows, mouth, or forehead furrows. Design an animal face on tagboard, cut out the shape, and staple on a stick, such as a tongue depressor, to make a mask that the child can hold like a fan. More complex masks may be inspired by consulting *Masks, Face Coverings, and Headgear* (Laliberte & Mogelon, 1973).

A beginning session in which you lead the pupils in expressing themselves through head, neck, arm, torso, and leg movements can free them to depict story actions with their bodies, since facial expressions cannot be seen. After modeling and practicing, allow the children free rein in expressing the story character's actions.

The role of masks in folklore is an interesting topic for research by individuals who are fascinated by *The Loon's Necklace* by William Toye, *Who's in Rabbit's House* by Verna Aardema, or other Indian and African tales. Masks play a significant role in Indian and African folklore.

Leo and Diane Dillon's illustrations for *Who's in Rabbit's House?*

depict the story as being performed by masked players. The model of that format can help the pupils develop their own ideas for dramatization and mask making.

## STORYTELLING

The oral tradition of folk literature should be perpetuated by young and old alike. Many children are fascinated by the drama of storytelling and are willing to spend the time needed to practice the tales. Children can be encouraged to tell the tales to class groups, the whole class, and perhaps other classes in the school. Telling the tales requires the ability to enunciate clearly and read expressively, using effective intonation, pitch, and stress to convey the message. See Chapter 7 for a description of the process that a teacher used with his class.

Many communities have storytelling groups. A local storyteller invited to entertain the class provides an enjoyable model for the children. A visiting storyteller may be willing to answer questions and give valuable tips for preparation of the storytelling experience.

I recommend that every teacher try storytelling. It requires practice but is well worth the effort. Prepare a familiar folktale for the first day of school. You develop a rapport with the class through eye contact and body language and your creative use of language that is different from reading aloud. Memorize key phrases to preserve the magic of folktale language, but word-for-word memorization is unnecessary. You will develop a storytelling style of your own. Three storytellers who share their techniques are Carolyn Feller Bauer (1977), Margaret MacDonald (1985), and Anne Pellowski (1984).

## MUSIC AND DANCE

Finding appropriate music to accompany storytelling becomes a challenging activity for the children after they understand that the author and illustrator are conveying a mood for the reader. Individuals can practice storytelling and set stories to music on cassette tapes to be shared with classmates. The prepared cassettes provide a classroom library for background music that can be used with storytelling, creative drama, and dance responses to literature.

Interpretive dance offers an expressive extension of folk literature. Begin by using excerpts from popular ballets and operettas that are musical renditions of folktales such as *The Sorcerer's Apprentice* or *Sleeping Beauty* (see Riordan, 1984). Encourage the children to move with the music, allowing the music to dictate their movements. The difference between dance and improvisation is that in dance one allows the music to dictate the movements. If the child takes the cues from the music, expressive dance becomes an individual interpretation of the story. Sources for teaching dance include books on dance and creative movement by Sue Leese (1980), Joan Russell (1975), and Carolyn Deitering (1980). Deitering's book deals specifically with the liturgical form of dance.

Knowledge of folk literature can enhance music appreciation. Composers have been inspired by folk literature to write beautiful classical music. One example is *The Firebird* composed as a ballet by Igor Stravinsky in 1910. Nine years later Stravinsky selected five excerpts from the ballet and entitled it, *The Firebird Suite*. From the five movements the listener can visualize the story: first, the "Introduction," which transports the listener to the fairyland; then, the haunting "Dance of the Firebird" when Prince Ivan released her from captivity, followed by a playful "Dance of the Princesses," the innocent captives of the evil Kastchei. Ivan's encounter with Kastchei is powerfully expressed in the fourth movement, the "Infernal Dance of King Kastchei." The "Finale" offers praise and gratitude for good overcoming evil and pays homage to Prince Ivan and his princess. When the ballet was presented for the first time in America, Maria Tallchief danced the role of the Firebird.

The story of Cinderella has been told frequently in music. The three works that have become classics are Rossini's Italian opera *La Cenerentola* (1817), Massenet's French opera *Cendrillon* (1899), and Prokofiev's Russian ballet *Zolushka* (1945).

## READER'S THEATER

Reader's theater provides creative oral reading within the classroom through two or more oral interpreters bringing a literature experience to an audience. Certain conventions are generally attended to by the participants:

1. The narrator and readers are seated on high stools or stand in a group in front of the audience.
2. Simple props may be used, but there is no use of scenery or costumes that takes the attention away from the oral interpretation.
3. The reader uses the voice to evoke mental images of characters and scenes.
4. The narrator speaks directly to the audience and does not interact with the other readers.
5. Each reader carries the script because the emphasis is on reading, not acting or memorization.
6. An effort is made to develop a personal relationship between the audience and the reader, with an emphasis on the sounds of the language.

Emphasis in classroom reader's theater is on using the voice to produce mental images of characters and scenes. Practicing with partners helps free the reader to develop dramatic expression.

Verna Aardema's books are especially adaptable for reader's theater because of the quantity of dialogue and repetitive ideophones. Nearly all folktales fit well into being rewritten for reader's theater production. The teacher and class can work together on writing the script, taking care to preserve the sounds of the language and the essential phrases while shortening the narrative to emphasize the individual reading parts. Third-grade classrooms at Collins School keep a file of prepared scripts for children to select. Groups of children chose the story they wished to perform and with minimal guidance developed their own interpretation, adding or omitting dialogue as they practiced (see Figure 6.2).

*Reader's Theater: Story Dramatization in the Classroom* by Shirlee Sloyer (1982) is a useful source of information for the teacher.


## PUPPETS

The sharply drawn characters of fairy tales and animal tales make wonderful puppets. From the simplest paper bag puppet to the most

**FIGURE 6.2**  Third-grade performance. Collins Forest Hills School, Grand Rapids, Michigan.

elaborate papier-mâché model, storybook characters can be easily identified by accentuating particular features. Hand, rod, or shadow puppets of princes, princesses, and witches can fit any favorite fairy tale. Simple silhouette figures can be joined with metal fasteners, moved with attached, thin sticks, and projected with an overhead projector; see *Play with Light and Shadow* by Herta Schonewolf (1968). Head puppets of tricksters like Anansi, Br'er Rabbit, Coyote, or Fox can be kept in the classroom for spontaneous dramatic plays of animal tales.

For puppet construction and stage ideas see *The Theatre Student and Puppetry: The Ultimate Disguise* by George Latshaw (1978). For learning hand puppet expression, consult *Making Puppets Come Alive* by Carol and Engler Fijan (1973).

Planning conversation for puppets and selecting background music to set the stage offer purposes for critical reading and rereading of the tales.

## VISUAL ART

The art in folk literature provides excellent models for children's artistic exploration. Together teacher and children can examine many books with quality illustrations. (In A Guide to Recommended Folk Literature, books with exemplary artwork are indicated with an asterisk.) After sharing folktale art, read unillustrated stories from collections such as Bierhorst's Native American stories (*The Girl Who Married a Ghost* and *The Naked Bear*), Finger's tales of South America (*Tales from Silver Lands*), and Harris's tales of Indian totems (*Once Upon a Totem* and *Once More upon a Totem*). Provide materials for experimenting with collage, cutting, printing, watercolor, and tempera painting. Encourage the children to choose media and colors that fit the mood of the story. This is good preparation for illustrating their own stories.

The middle-school international literature unit described in Chapter 2 began with reading from their large library collection of folk literature. Art activities by the middle-school students included book covers featuring the country and characters, collages about the story, the country, the customs, and the characters, and murals illustrating plot and sequence of the stories.

The third-grade fairy tale unit at Forest Hills Collins Public School, Grand Rapids, Michigan, ended with a program, "Open Castle of the Thirds." Family and friends were invited "to celebrate the joy of fairy tales, reader's theater, and castle architecture of our enchanted third-graders" (note on invitation). During the fairy tale study, the children became intrigued with castles. David Macaulay's *Castle* (1977) helped them understand the reality of the structures. Groups of five worked together to build their own castle for their imaginary kingdom (see Figure 6.3). Some castles were completely built from recycled materials, adding ecological awareness to their study.

The fairy tale study was integrated with a social studies unit. The map skills and geographic terms introduced in the third-grade curriculum were taught within the context of the imaginary kingdoms. Each child planned and drew a fairy tale continent and labeled bays, peninsulas, mountains, deserts, and lakes. Their continent had to include at least one country, two states, and two cities. Each drawing

**FIGURE 6.3**  Katie sets up her group's castle made of recycled materials.

had a key to the kingdom (see Figure 6.4). They studied heraldry and made their own family shields. The school corridor, decorated as an entrance to a castle, gave visual evidence of learning. Displays of the artwork included their own stories with lavish book cover designs. Videos were taken while the children were working, and viewing these was a popular part of the final celebration.

For instructions for using various media, consult Laura Chapman's series, *Discover Art* (1984). *Paper Sculpture* by Pauline Johnson (1964) illustrates simple techniques for making such creations as dioramas, murals, and paper costumes.

## VISUAL IMAGERY

Some children are not aware that they see pictures in their mind. Building this awareness helps the children relate new ideas to concepts already in their experience. Talking about visual images helps

**FIGURE 6.4**  Third-graders used their map skills to create fairy kingdoms.

children who are better at imagery than at verbal communication to express their ideas.

Since visual imagery is not commonly described as a creative activity, a specific lesson is described here for developing the reader's ability to picture ideas in response to literature.

**LESSON OBJECTIVE:**  To develop awareness that words can create a picture in your mind.

**MATERIAL:**  *The Fisherman and His Wife,* a Grimm tale translated by Randell Jarrell, or any folktale using vivid descriptions or depicting vivid actions.

**PROCEDURE:**

1. Explain to the children that storytellers use words to create pictures. Try an experiment to show that many words create pictures in our minds. Ask the children to think about what they see when you say a word. Use words that you know are in their experience (e.g., *baby, man, woman*). Ask for a description of what they see.

2. Suggest that while listening to the story you are going to read, they pay attention to the kinds of pictures they see in their minds.
3. After the reading, ask for responses, based on the general pictures they received.
4. Focus on certain expressions or statements, such as

> . . . and when he came to the sea, the water was all violet and dark blue and gray and not so green and yellow any more, but it was still calm. (1980, p. 7)
> The sea was all black and thick, and began to boil up from underneath so that it threw up bubbles, and a whirlwind passed over it. (1980, p. 12)
> . . . and outside a storm was raging. (1980, p. 23)

5. Use as many of the following as you sense are appropriate for your group:
   a. Describe the most important thing in your mind picture.
   b. Describe the background of your mind picture (be sure to include color).
   c. What is light in the picture? What is dark?
   d. What is moving? What is still?

## EXPLORING LANGUAGE

Creative response to the language of the folktale enhances growth in reading ability. Sensory involvement beyond the visual and the auditory helps the reader become totally involved in the reading. The following two lessons are offered at the simplest level to encourage creative planning.

**LESSON OBJECTIVE:** To recognize that words can provoke appeal to taste, touch, and smells.
**MATERIAL:** A favorite folktale, such as *Mazel and Shlimazel,* retold by Isaac Bashevis Singer; chart paper.
**PROCEDURE:**
1. Have children list words that make them want to taste, touch, or smell something.
2. Select a book that you have read before, so that upon second reading the listeners can concentrate on their feelings.

**3.** Brainstorm words and phrases for the chart. Ask children to explain why they have chosen those words.

For a reinforcing activity, post a large wall chart. From independent reading, children can write words on the chart. Include book title and page number.

**LESSON OBJECTIVE:**   To delight in the expression of words as the reader makes the sounds.

**MATERIAL:**   An alliterative tale, such as *Bringing the Rain to Kapiti Plain,* retold by Verna Aardema, or *One Fine Day* by Nonny Hogrogian.

**PROCEDURE:**

**1.** Read the story.
**2.** Encourage children to chant the refrains and express their feeling through body movement.
**3.** Repeat, and enjoy as often as you can.

This experience will help children become more word conscious and extend their use of story structure by developing a sense of the rhyme and rhythm of language.

Creative response to word origins can change a routine study of the history of the English language into a captivating study. The egocentric nature of children leads them to believe that language originated in their native tongue, which always existed. Discovering words in the folk literature that originated in other languages can help children establish a more accurate historic understanding of language.

Not all children are intrigued by word origins, so an enthusiastic teacher is needed to encourage them to learn about this subject as an independent challenge. Once children have become interested in word study through exploration of vocabulary in myths and legends, that interest may carry over into other areas.

Mythology offers a good beginning for word study because so many words in every European language derive from Greek and Roman mythology. After Christianity spread throughout the world, educated persons no longer believed the Greek myths, but they continued to read the great literature that was filled with mythological figures and exploits. Words derived from myths were introduced in various languages when new words were coined. Many of those words are recognizable by prefix or root in the English language of today.

Scientists drew on mythological terminology to name new animals and plants, new chemical and phenomenal discoveries. The Latin or Greek term gave a universality to the new name that made it understandable across many languages. A valuable source of information for discovering the role of myths in the history of language is *Words from the Myths* by Isaac Asimov (1961).

Independent discovery of word origins can proceed from word to story, or from story to word. Both strategies are demonstrated here.

LESSON OBJECTIVE:   To discover word origins.
MATERIAL:   Bulletin board; color-coded cards.
PROCEDURE:

FROM WORD TO STORY

1. Encourage children by example and discussion to search out word sources.
2. Post an attractive bulletin board on the classroom wall or in a learning center and invite individual participation (see Figure 6.5).
3. Specialized lists can be used, such as science words (Arctic Ocean, Atlas, brontosaurus, fauna, flora, helium, planet, plutonium, solar, territory, and uranium) or everyday phrases (Achilles heel; by Jove; Midas touch; work like a Trojan).

FROM STORY TO WORD

1. Tell the children that when they come to a word in a myth or legend that they have heard somewhere else with another meaning, they should look it up in the dictionary. They should check to see if the origin of the word is given.
2. Prepare color-coded cards for the children to use in posting their findings on the bulletin board. They should put the name of the story where the word was found on a card of one color, the word itself on a card of a second color, and its modern meaning on a card of a third color. These cards should be lined up in columns under appropriate headings (Story, Word, Modern Meaning).

FIGURE 6.5   Discovering word origins: A model for a bulletin board display.

```
              WHAT'S THE CONNECTION?

Find out                              Words We Use
1.  Where did that word come from?       cosmos
2.  What special meaning                 chaos
    of the first word led                echo
    to making the                        extraterrestrial
    new word?                            giant
3.  If possible, name a myth or          hero
    legend from folk literature          hygiene
    that uses the word                   ocean
    in its original form.                siren
                                         zephyr
```

```
On this part of the board the children will write
the findings from researching the word, answering
the questions above.

Sources children could use:
Words from Myths
Webster's New World Dictionary, or
another classroom dictionary
```

## SUMMARY

Creative response to folk literature can take many forms: creative drama, mask making, storytelling, music, reader's theater, puppetry, the visual arts, and language exploration. Specific teaching suggestions are given for visual imagery and language exploration. For the other creative responses, the information in this book is limited to the relationship between folk literature and the activity. Sources are suggested for information pertinent to implementing the activities.

Each activity suggested is, by itself, worthy of merit. In addition, the extent to which the children respond through the activity gives the teacher an indication of how completely the children have understood the characters, story line, and theme of the literature they have read. Interpretation for creative response requires critical thinking about the reading.

# 7

# A Fifth-Sixth Grade Class
# Uses Folk Literature

This chapter is an account of an actual classroom use of folk literature in a reading and writing program. The class is a combined fifth
and sixth grade in Beckwith Public School, Grand Rapids, Michigan. The teacher is John Booy.

## TALES AND TOTEM POLES

Jill, Katie, and Kathi carried their brightly decorated five-foot
totem down the hall from their classroom to the third-grade class
(see Figure 7.1). The third-graders were sitting on the floor, eagerly
awaiting the visit, for the large totems had been very visible in the
art room. The girls placed the totem in front of the class and sat
cross-legged next to it. They proceeded to tell their original, well-
rehearsed stories, following an Indian tradition. Jill began:

> The first story in this series starts at the top of the family
> totem pole with Gomokish and his tale of the unicorn. He is the
> great-grandfather of the totem.
> Next comes Naway, the grandfather of the totem, and his
> exciting legend of the bear and the salmon.
> The father of the boy who carved this pole, Iracian, has a
> wonderful story of himself and the beautiful pelican.
> The carver of the totem pole symbolizes the earth in his sec-
> tion for he learned the importance of respect for nature.

**FIGURE 7.1**
Jill, Katie, and Kathi are ready to follow the Indian storytelling tradition with a visit to the third grade.

Kathi told her story:

### HOW THE RAINBOW AFFECTED UNICORNS
### WITH THE HELP OF GOMOKISH

One beautiful sunny day in the 1600s, my tribe the Shoshone were all going about our own business, when an old Unicorn, I'd say has been living for at least 15 years, came trotting onto our land looking so much in pain.

Then I, Gomokish, noticed his leg. It was bleeding and he was limping on it. I ran over to him and picked the Unicorn up, gently, and took him to the river to clean the cut out.

"Oh, you poor thing, I will help you." I remember saying. "I will help you."

The Unicorn sort of looked up at me, in a way knowing that I would. I walked from there to the forest trying to find the right leaf to help him. A tree that had a soft, but not brittle leaf that would wrap around its leg to protect the bruise. I know that there should be a tree for him, because Oregon has tons of trees.

When I found one I carefully wrapped the leaf around the Unicorn's cut and took him to my home.

Each day the Unicorn was getting better. I would help it walk and I knew by the way he cooperated with me he very much appreciated it.

When the day came to let the Unicorn go, it was very hard on me.

"Little fellow, it's time for you to go."

That's all I said, then I turned around and left, wondering if the Unicorn was going to be happy or not.

A few days after the Unicorn left Oregon, he was trotting happily in the woods, catching some of the last few raindrops, on his pure white fur shaded with brown.

The Unicorn came upon a rainbow while he was walking, and remembering how poor he was, started to climb it, wanting to reach the end for the pot of gold. Once he was in the middle, the Unicorn stopped to take a look around to see the Earth.

The Unicorn turned on the rainbow, trying to get a good look, but he slipped, because of his slippery hooves, and tumbled down the rainbow to where he first started from.

He started to climb it again, but whenever he reached the middle and stopped to take a look around, he would end up where he started from.

The Unicorn knew that if he would just not stop in the middle then he would make it to the end, but he could not bear not stopping to take a look.

When he finally stopped trying to climb the rainbow, and went home, he noticed that the colors of the rainbow had rubbed off on him, so he went to the river to wash off.

When he was done and went back to his home he still had the colors on his horn, so he went back to wash it off, but the colors wouldn't rub off. He scrubbed and scrubbed but nothing would come off.

The Unicorn was one of the oldest ones living, and because of what happened to him all the other Unicorns received the colors of the rainbow on their horns too.

The Unicorn went back to Oregon to see me, Gomokish. I saw him coming, and knew him because of the rainbow on his horn. We both know it was happy and peaceful sign.

Jill told her story, which concerned the middle section of the totem pole:

### HOW THE SALMON CAME TO THE WILLAMETTE RIVER

At one time the Shoshone tribe was happy. They lived in a beautiful place with plenty of food and led good lives.

Then something changed. The people became greedy and selfish and soon food became scarce.

The people grew too lazy to hunt so they took the easy task of fishing.

Soon all the big red fish called salmon were gone and there was not a fish left in the stream.

The people began to starve and many died.

A boy called Naway saw the grief of his tribe, but he was happy.

For long ago his parents died and his tribe made him an outcast. He went to live in the forest with a kind old bear he called Nicka.

She provided his food and shelter and the love his mother would have given him.

He knew the people had caused this trouble.

When he returned home that night he said to Nicka, "I must find a way to help my people even though it is they that have brought this upon themselves."

"Yes, my son, I have taught you many powerful secrets. I am sure you'll know which one is best," the old bear replied.

For three days Naway worked on a clay fish. When it was finished he painted it red and it looked like a salmon.

Nicka saw it and chanted her medicine song and told Naway to fetch some water in one of the deerskin bags.

When he returned, his mother, Nicka, put the "fish" in the water and it became alive.

Together they brought it to the stream and let it go.

As the fish dove into the water its number kept multiplying until nearly one hundred fish were in the water.

Naway was proud of his mother for this was the greatest magic the old bear had ever performed.

Nicka told the boy that he must preach to his people and tell them about the fish and that they must respect the land.

She added, "I will come and kill the village if my laws are not obeyed."

Naway turned and started toward his village. The people were surprised to see him, but listened to his story.

Naway began, "My people, you have taken all the red fish out of the river and now you are dying."

"My mother, Nicka, the great bear and I have given you more fish for your river. Those fish belong to all, nature and our people.

"You must never do this again, it has hurt you and the animals.

"If you turn lazy and disrespectful ever again the red ones will leave your streams never to return.

"But more deathly to you, my peaceful Nicka will come here and kill you all for disobeying her laws!"

The people gazed in horror but praised Naway for returning their fish.

From then on the Shoshone have always held the fish in great honor.

The bear was made sacred and Naway was made chief of the tribe.

The salmon have stayed in the Willamette River and still today the Indians dance the fish dance in honor of the salmon.

Katie pointed to the bottom picture on the totem as she began her storytelling:

### THE PELICAN GOD

Long ago there was a tribe called the Shoshones.

Every morning the men of the tribe would leave their home and go to a nearby river to catch some fish.

When they came back the women of the tribe would have a fire ready to cook the large amounts of fish the men had caught.

One morning the men started down toward the river as usual. When they got there they sat and sat with their fishing sticks moving ever slightly by the fall breeze. All day long they sat but no catch.

"There is no fish in this river. Today we come home with nothing," said a tribe member named Iracian.

"Yes, we will starve," said Rackson.

The men started home with empty sacks.

That night everyone was showered over [with] grief. The fires set off a soft glow just enough so you could see the weary faces among the circle. There were streaks of tears across the cheeks of the tribe members.

The fear of starvation swelled up into everyone. The days that passed were the hardest of all.

Still, the men went to the river in the morning then returned when darkness fell. Every night was the same, no fish.

People began to get very hungry, some died and some remained ill.

One night as the Shoshones gathered around the fire, Iracian spoke:

"I know we are all hungry. The fish must've left us, without telling us why. We must have a dance for food tomorrow night or else we will perish. It has to be big and meaningful, if that doesn't work we are hopeless."

The next night a fire crackled in the middle of the circle. Many men were dressed in bright earthly colors.

They danced to the beat of the drums, while the rest of the tribe sang Indian songs.

Soon it ended.

"Now we must wait, we must sleep," Iracian said tiredly.

More days passed and still no sight of food. While the men were out at the river the women scavenged around looking for plants to eat. When they did find some, they were very small, and could not be shared among the whole Shoshone group.

"I see we are all dying of starvation, so I plan to go on a journey in quest of the Pelican God. Surely he will give us food and send the fish back. Then we can live healthy again," said the only brave soul, Iracian.

The next day Iracian set out on his journey.

It was spring so he had no fear of storms. But on the second day a storm came about. Iracian quickly wrapped himself up in his bear furs. His braided black hair blew wildly in the wind. His bare feet cut sharply on the jagged rocks and pieces of twigs, leaving drips of blood behind.

The animals above and below scurried away to shelter. Iracian quickened his pace until finally he came to a cliff covered with heather. There was a dark cave nearby and Iracian knew that the Pelican was in there.

"Hello, Pelican God," called Iracian.

"Come in, Iracian, I have been expecting you," said the Pelican God. "Let's see, you are here because your tribe is suffering of starvation, because the fish in the river have left you. Am I right?"

Iracian nodded his head.

"You have come here also to ask me for fish and ask me where the fish went off to."

"Yes," said Iracian quietly.

"Well, the fish went to a different lake. They wanted a tribe who only fished for what they needed. Your people seemed to fish for more than you needed and filled yourselves so full of fish so often that the fish didn't want to fight for their life every single day." The Pelican's green eyes glared at Iracian while his long orange beak remained shut for some time.

Finally he nodded his big white feathery head and stood on his humanlike body flapping his wings. He walked around Iracian, he took each stop with caution as if Iracian would try something.

"Okay, Iracian. I will make the fish go back only if you take what you need and go right now to apologize to the King Fish."

Once again Iracian started out on a long journey to the land of the fish.

When we got there he saw many fish swimming around the King Fish, who was sitting on a lily pad. Iracian went over to the fish.

"King Fish," he began, "I am sorry about the fish in our river. I'm Iracian, of the Shoshones. We are all starving because of the fish leaving us. Please bring them back, for we will only take what we need," he pleaded.

"Are you sure?" said the King Fish, "My young fish were very angry at your tribe."

"Yes, King Fish," said Iracian.

"Okay, I will let the fish back in."

That night Iracian returned home, with good news. The people were waiting patiently for Iracian to tell them.

That night the men went fishing for an hour, then returned home with a sack of fish. The tribe had a dance of thankfulness. They ate and rejoiced. But they only took what they needed.

## UNDERSTANDING THE STORY

What preceded this final production? It all began with one reading group. They had finished a basal reader, and the teacher felt that they had been reading in a very mechanical fashion, without really thinking about the content of stories. Before starting the next basal, he decided to introduce legends and myths and encourage each group member to read independently. He was able to gather about sixty of the titles suggested in A Guide to Recommended Folk Literature for Children, and the children began comparing the various legends.

During reading group time Mr. Booy taught story mapping, categorizing, and recognizing conflict and theme development, using the lesson suggestions in Chapters 3 and 4 of this book. The children were most interested in comparing Native American tales with those from other cultures, and the study proceeded in that direction. The children never seemed to tire of mapping the stories.

During this time children wrote journal entries and made comparison charts and story maps to share with the group. Meanwhile, the rest of the class asked to be included, and the teacher began reading Native American legends and myths to the whole group. The artwork of the books was intriguing to the children and the class embarked on a study of Native American art.

## REINFORCING UNDERSTANDING

Earlier in the school year the class had studied trees. Now they became interested in trees as symbols and the Indian totems became very real to them. With the cooperation of the art teacher, the children planned to build their own totems. The class was divided into groups of three, and they began constructing their shapes from the scores of boxes the teacher collected from local merchants. Each one in the group of three picked one object to place on the pole, which they would later write about. Kathi picked the unicorn, Jill chose the salmon, and Katie chose the pelican.

Drawings of possible shapes and design were made on paper before the actual construction began. When the groups of three were satisfied with their plans, they began taping the boxes together, often reconstructing the boxes to fit their planned shapes. Much masking tape was used! Then the papier-mâché process began, a slow but inexpensive activity, with the use of brown paper toweling for the surface layer. The designs that the children had drawn on paper were now drawn with pencil on the totem, and painted with black paint. The final step was to add the color (see Figure 7.2). The use of the textured paper toweling made it possible to leave some of the surface a barklike brown. The whole process took three months, with much of the work fitting into spare moments, recess, and lunch breaks.

**FIGURE 7.2**  Each symbol on the totem was created and constructed by the children.

## WRITING WITH FOLK LITERATURE

Meanwhile, prewriting activities were leading up to the students writing their own legends to accompany the totems. The rereading of several short legends focused on types of characters, names of characters, common themes, and common conflicts. The picturesque and flowing language was noted. The day before the "serious writing" was going to begin, the groups spent an afternoon researching the Indian tribe or area that they had chosen to write about. This was to verify what they had learned from the legends concerning the location, type of environment, habits, and animals of the region. Although this was not their favorite activity, the children recognized that the aura of a legend had to be established.

Now they were ready to plan their plot, conflict, theme, and characters to explain the object that they were designing on their totems. Story mapping served as an outline for their stories. They were very familiar with the process from mapping other authors' stories, and now they used this skill to plan what they were going to write. For example, Jill prepared the map shown in Figure 7.3 before writing her story. The teacher stated that this was a very helpful step in the writing process. The map helped the writers maintain the flow of their stories, which took several sittings to complete.

Children refined their stories by reading them to the other group members and receiving suggestions from them. The teacher edited, and met with each child for final revisions during independent work time.

Now came the most difficult part, in which the students would prepare their own stories for telling. Mr. Booy found that the step from writing to reading the stories was not too difficult, but telling the story in an animated, interesting manner was a big order for fifth- and sixth-graders. They proceeded to work through the following six steps:

1. The writer memorized his or her own story.
2. The writer read the story to a partner line by line and the partner recited the line with exaggerated expression.
3. The teacher modeled, telling a story using nonsense words, and asked the class to determine what the story was about by reading his gestures and voice intonations. Several children of-

TITLE   "How the Salmon Came to the Willamette River"

SETTING   Where:   A forest in Oregon
          When:    1880s
          Who:     Shoshone Indians
                   Nicka--the bear
                   Red One--the salmon
                   Naway--the Indian boy who lives
                        with the bear

PROBLEM:   The Shoshone fish all the salmon out of the
Willamette River.  Naway, who has lived with the bear
since his parents died, tries to help.

RESOLUTION:   Naway makes a clay fish and with Nicka's
special powers he makes it come alive and puts it into
the river where it produces 100 fish.  Naway makes the
people realize that if they ever destroy the fish
again the bear will kill them all.

ACTIONS:   1.   The Shoshone fish all the fish out of the
                Willamette River.  The bear and boy see
                it.
           2.   The boy makes a clay fish and the bear
                transforms it into a living fish.
           3.   The bear puts it into the river where it
                turns into many fish.
           4.   Naway preaches to the people never to
                fish all fish out of the river again or
                the Red One will never return.

**FIGURE 7.3**  Jill's story map for her legend.

fered to tell their story using nonsense words and gestures, to
practice animated telling.

4. Each group listened to other groups practice the story.
5. The groups told their stories to the class, and the class commented on clarity, pace, and use of gestures.
6. The groups told their stories and displayed their totem in another classroom. Only groups that passed the approval of the class could take their stories to another room.

All the groups eventually received approval from the class, and the whole school was enriched by the accomplishments of the fifth- and sixth-graders. Kevin, Nicole, and Scott brought their stories to the second grade (see Figure 7.4). Each of them wrote about different tribes, rather than sharing stories about one tribe. The teacher re-

**FIGURE 7.4**
Kevin and Nicole set up
their totem in grade two
for a story-telling
session.

ported that Kevin was a fifth-grader who that year advanced in learning more than any other child in the class. Here is his story:

### THE MOON OWL

Long ago, in Cleveland, there was a forest. The name of the
forest was called the Changwa forest because there was an Indian village in it with the Changwa Indians living there. The
forest had many animals in it. Most of the animals were birds. It
had loons, ducks, eagles, hawks. But one bird was quite different from all the others. This bird was the owl.

The reason the owl was so different from all the other birds was because he was always wondering about things. Each morning he would wake up wondering about something.

One time he woke up wondering about something a little different than all the other things he worried about. He was wondering about the sky. He wondered why the sky was always brightly lit during the daytime but was dark and didn't have a light in it at night.

This puzzled all the other birds too. They decided that they should do something about it.

They all thought and thought about lighting the sky at night. Then they decided to have someone wash in the river of light. Then they could build a throne for that bird to sit on, high in the sky.

The birds thought this was a wonderful idea, but who would do it? This, too, puzzled the birds until they agreed to let the owl who first got them into this do it.

So the owl flew high into the sky and then dove down all the way down to the bottom of the river of light. When he came back up, he was a new bird. The other birds decided to name him The Moon.

They tried out their moon that night. It worked! When the owl came back from his work, he slept all day.

That is still his schedule today. Working at night, lighting the sky, and sleeping during the day.

When asked for an evaluation of the experience, John Booy reported that he felt all the time devoted to this was worthwhile.

"No time was spent on pencil biting or staring into space," he reported. "By the time the legend writing began, the children had been saturated with Indian lore, and they didn't seem to tire of it."

He could see improvement in other writing the children were doing. They appeared to be more comfortable with writing assignments, and expressed themselves in writing more effectively than before the legend-writing experience. They continued to be avid readers, finding more folk literature, as well as books from other genres, in the library.

# A Guide
# to Recommended Folk
# Literature for Children

The books presented in this guide meet MacDonald's (1979) guidelines for evaluation of literary versions of folktales and the standards of the American Folklore Society (see Chapter 1). All of the tales used in the lesson plans are included here. Each book that tells one single tale is listed alphabetically by the name of the person who retold, translated, or adapted the story. The collections of folktales are listed alphabetically by the editor or compiler of the volumes. An asterisk preceding an entry indicates that the book's illustrations are worthy of note. If no illustrator is named, the author is the illustrator.

The appraisal for each folktale includes a brief summary of the theme or the plot of individual stories, or information about the content of stories in the collections. The country or origin of the tale is given. Suggestions are given for using the selection in the classroom, or a reference is made to an outstanding feature of the story. Generally, no recommendation is given as to the appropriate grade level for using the story because I believe that decision is a personal one to be made by the child, teacher, or librarian. The multidimensionality of folktales makes them appropriate at a variety of age and grade levels.

*Aardema, Verna. (1981). *Bringing the rain to Kapiti Plain*. Illustrated by Beatriz Vidal. New York: Dial. [African]

This version of a tale from Kenya adds a cumulative refrain and the rhythm of "The House that Jack Built." The story structure supplies a framework for story writing. The repetition and picturesque language make this a favorite for reading aloud and chanting. The brilliant folk art illustrations set the mood for the inevitable rainstorm.

*Aardema, Verna. (1979). *The riddle of the drum: A tale from Tizapan, Mexico*. Illustrated by Tony Chen. New York: Four Winds Press. [Mexican]

Prince Tuzan meets swift runner Corrin Corran, archer Tirin Tiran, hearer Oyin Oyan, blower Soplin Soplan, and eater Comin Comon. All help the prince solve the riddle and perform other feats to win the princess. This hero tale of enchantment is a model of language patterning. Compare Prince Tuzan with the prince in Boris Zvorykin's *The Firebird* (Russian) and with the warrior in Robert SanSouci's *The Legend of Scarface* (Native American).

*Aardema, Verna. (1977). *Who's in rabbit's house?* Illustrated by Leo & Diane Dillon. New York: Dial. [African]

The Masai African tale, illustrated with actors wearing animal masks, is a good model for dramatization. The jackal, leopard, elephant, and rhinoceros offer unsuitable help for rabbit, who tries to get the fearful creature out of his house. All are surprised at the identity of the occupant. Language patterns, use of repetition, and ideophones make this version appealing for oral reading and chanting.

*Aardema, Verna. (1975). *Why mosquitoes buzz in people's ears*. Illustrated by Leo & Diane Dillon. New York: Dial. [African]

When King Lion calls a tribal council to see why Mother Owl doesn't wake the Sun, he finds a chain of blame sent from monkey (who killed baby owl) to crow to rabbit to python to iguana to mosquito. An agreement to punish mosquito satisfies Mother Owl, and the days follow their normal pattern once more. The pattern of language is noteworthy and can be chanted by the audience when read aloud. The dramatic full-color illustrations won the Caldecott award.

Adams, E. B. (1983). *Korean Cinderella*. Illustrated by Dong Ho Choi. Seoul, Korea: Seoul International Tourist Publishing. [Korean]

> Kongjee is the beautiful, talented stepdaughter who is given impossible jobs to finish. Magical help appears in the form of a black cow (not indigenous to Korea) when her hoe breaks on the rocks; a toad who closes the hole in the water jar; birds who hull the rice; and a weaving maid from beyond the Milky Way who makes Kongjee a dress for her uncle's wedding. On the way to the wedding, Kongjee jumps out of the way of the new governor and loses her shoe. He finds Kongjee and is captivated by her "modesty and sincerity" and "her beauty, filial obedience and charm." The text is written in English and Korean on each page.

Aesop. (1985). *Aesop's fables*. Selected and illustrated by Michael Hague. New York: Holt, Rinehart & Winston. [European]

> Simple, lilting language characterizes this collection of thirteen tales. Each has the moral stated. To develop critical thinking, state the moral before reading the story and ask the children to listen for the events that teach the lesson.

Aesop. (1981). *Aesop's fables*. Illustrated by Heidi Holder. New York: Viking Kestrel. [European]

> The nine fables in this collection include both common and seldom-heard fables from reputable sources. The elegant, ornate language offers a good vocabulary builder for the intermediate-grade reader who already knows the fables. The delicate watercolor drawings alternate between fantasy scenes and realistic animals, offering interesting points of comparison. This version will challenge the advanced reader and offer practice in interpreting the message.

*Aesop. (1989). *Aesop's Fables*. Selected and illustrated by Lisbeth Zwerger. Saxonville, MA: Picture Book Studio.

> Lisbeth Zwerger, recipient of the 1990 Hans Christian Andersen award for distinguished illustration, offers whimsical, humorous characters in her interpretation of the familiar fables. The distinctive watercolors extend the text and offer hints for children's predictions of what the moral will be. The language is clear and the

moral is stated at the end. The twelve fables include the most common ones plus "The Moon and Her Mother" (nothing ever suits one who is always changing) and "The Monkey and the Camel" (seeking popularity is the fastest way to lose friends).

*Baker, Olaf. (1981). *Where the buffaloes begin*. Illustrated by Stephen Gammell. New York: Frederick Warne. [Native American]
Nawa, the wise Indian, was the voice that kept the legend alive. The beautiful language in this version of a Plains Indian tale captures the sights and sounds of the prairie. The black-and-white sketches enhance the reader's impression of the revered animals and the vastness of the plains. Discuss the Indian regard for the buffalo.

Bang, Molly Garrett. (1976). *Wiley and the Hairy Man*. New York: Macmillan. [Regional American]
If the Hairy Man can be fooled three times, he will never bother anyone again. Wiley and his mother work hard to find ways to outwit the Hairy Man. Wiley conquers his fear, confronts the Hairy Man, and proves that people can outwit evil through wisdom and caring for one another. The interesting, easy writing style makes this a favorite for independent reading.

Baylor, Byrd. (1976). *And it is still that way*. New York: Scribners. [Native American]
The introduction describes how the legends in the book were collected from Arizona Indian children at school. Baylor has written down the stories exactly as the Native American children remembered hearing them from their parents and grandparents. They are grouped into topics: "Why Animals Are the Way They Are," "Why Our World Is as It Is," "Great Troubles and Great Heroes," "People Can turn into Anything," "Brother Coyote," "Magic All Around Us." This collection provides a model for children recording family folklore.

Baylor, Byrd. (1981). *A god on every mountain top*. Illustrated by Carol Brown. New York: Scribners. [Native American]
Byrd Baylor presents a collection of myths and legends from various Native American tribes. The first two sections, "Begin-

nings" and "Changes," contain the myths. Legends comprise the remaining sections: "Power," "Magic," "Mystery and Dreams," "The Beings in the Mountains." Discuss tribal beliefs that the Native Americans pass on to their children and the importance of the environment to the Native Americans.

★Bernstein, Margery, & Kobrin, Janet. (1976). *The first morning: An African myth.* Illustrated by Enid Warner Romanek. New York: Scribners. [African]

A tale of the Sukuma people of East Africa begins with earth animals living in darkness. Lion has seen the light in the sky during a storm. Outwitting the Sky King, the mouse, fly, and spider take the box of light back and are surprised to find in it a rooster. Then the rooster "calls up the sun." The story illustrates the need to suspend judgment throughout the narrative and to add one's own interpretation to the ending.

★Bernstein, Margery, & Kobrin, Janet. (1977). *The summer maker: An Ojibway Indian myth.* Illustrated by Anne Burgess. New York: Scribners. [Native American]

Ojeeg the fisher and his animal friends go to the land above the mountain to find summer. A manitou tells them to crack open a hole in the sky and let the birds out. They succeed with difficulty, and complications arise. Note the human characteristics of Ojeeg, the otter. Compare with *How Summer Came to Canada* by William Toye.

Bierhorst, John. (1978). *The girl who married a ghost and other tales from the North American Indian.* Photos by Edward S. Curtis. New York: Four Winds Press. [Native American]

An authentic collection of North American Indian tales is illustrated with beautifully reproduced photographs from writer-explorer Edward Curtis. Nine stories portray each major region inhabited by North American Indians. Types of stories include origin myths, wonder stories, ghost stories, and trickster animal tales. The photographs provide a link between the reality of the Indians' homes and activities and the mythical tales. Bierhorst captures Indian thought in his narrative, and his style challenges the sophisticated reader.

Bierhorst, John, editor. (1987). *The naked bear: Folktales of the Iroquois*. Illustrated by Dirk Zimmer. New York: Morrow. [Native American]

> The sixteen folktale versions in this collection were translated from the Seneca language. Each figure of speech and detail of plot had its origin in the native language, abridged and recombined by Bierhorst to offer enjoyable stories of romance and adventure. The stories show European influence but also variants of tales told by other Native American tribes. Legendary characters include cannibal ogres, Naked Bear and Stone Coats, trickster turtle, and hunters married to animal wives. End notes help in identification of motifs shared with other tales.

*Bierhorst, John. (1978). *The ring in the prairie*. Illustrated by Leo & Diane Dillon. New York: Dial. [Native American]

> Originally set down by Henry Schoolcraft, this legend is in the poetic tradition of Native American folklore. Hunter Waupee is intrigued by a strange circle in the prairie grass, and supernatural events begin. Legendary motifs include humans changing to animals, marriage of human with supernatural being, and use of charms. Poetic language and imagery is exemplary for language study.

*Bierhorst, John. (1984). *Spirit child*. Illustrated by Barbara Cooney. New York: Morrow. [Mexican]

> Bierhorst translated an Aztec account of the birth of Christ. This version interweaves Biblical stories, medieval legend, and traditional Aztec lore. The illustrations emulate Aztec art in a striking manner. Compare with the Bible story of the birth of Jesus.

*Blackmore, Vivien. (1984). *Why corn is golden: Stories about plants*. Illustrated by Susana Martinez-Ostos. Boston: Little, Brown. [Mexican]

> This is a rare collection of short, comical, magical tales from old Mexico. Some come from old Mexican Indian tribes and others from the time of Spanish soldiers and missionaries. The immediate sources were people in the countryside and anthropological collections. Each story begins with a statement that hints at the

explanation for the plant's existence. A portrait made of plants gives the answers to six riddles of the folk.

★Brown, Marcia. (1961). *Once a mouse*. New York: Scribner. [East Indian]
Marcia Brown tells this fable from ancient India using woodcuts and simple narrative. The old hermit reflects about big and little. When the mouse is changed to cat, dog, and then to tiger, he forgets his humble beginning. The message can be understood at different levels of complexity depending on the developmental level of the reader. Can be used to demonstrate understanding of theme.

Brown, Marcia. (1947; 1989). *Stone soup*. New York: Scribner. [French]
This popular, classic tale has been enjoyed by generations of children. The simple story of soldiers changing the attitude of the townspeople from fear to friendliness captures the delight of both young and old readers. The book offers a natural script for dramatizing and a recipe for classroom cooking.

Bryan, Ashley. (1977). *The dancing granny*. New York: Atheneum. [Central American]
Spider Anase uses his clever trickery to get Granny Anika to dance away from her field so he can feed his family from her garden. Introduce this book to children who already know the African Anansi. This version, which is from the Antilles, depicts the spider as a young man, whereas in African tales he is a spider man or an old man.

★Bryan, Ashley. (1986). *Lion and the ostrich chicks*. New York: Atheneum. [African]
These four tales from different parts of Africa must be read aloud to celebrate the wonderful sounds of language captured by Ashley Bryan. The stories should be read slowly and expressively so that the listeners can sense the alliteration and interior rhyme that cause a flow of sound. The children can join in and repeat the recurring rhymes, such as in "Lion and the Ostrich Chicks" and

"Jackal's Favorite Game." It is not necessary to explain the unusual words because the children sense the meaning from the story structure. The illustrations are painted with oils to resemble African carvings.

*Bryan, Ashley. (1971). *The ox of the wonderful horns and other African tales*. New York: Atheneum. [African]
> The five stories include four trickster animal and one fairy tale. The stories are excellent short stories to use in teaching theme. The trickster animals are the frog, the hare, and the spider. All of these are admired by Africans for their cunning. Make charts to compare trickster traits. Provide other trickster tales for independent reading.

*Bryan, Ashley. (1989). *Turtle knows your name*. New York: Atheneum. [West Indian]
> Up-sili-mana Tum-pa-lerado is the little boy's long name that was so hard to remember but so easy to pronounce. The boy goes on a search to find out his granny's name, and she goes out to discover who told him. This is a delightful story to chant with young listeners. The repeated language sounds and rhymes and the humorous story line make this a favorite to read and reread with beginning readers. Compare this West Indian tale with the Chinese "Tikki tikki tembo."

*Caduto, Michael, & Bruchac, Joseph. (1988). *Keepers of the earth*. Illustrated by J. K. Fadden & C. Wood. Golden, CO: Fulcrum. [Native American]
> This extraordinary book features a collection of Native American tales with related environmental activities. The stories are presented as a treasure from people who respected the earth and as a link between our imagination and our surroundings. The first two chapters, a guide for using and enjoying the book, offer specific tips for storytelling and strategies for using the science teaching ideas in each chapter. The carefully chosen tales are categorized by topics: creation, fire, geology, wind and weather, water, sky, astronomy, seasons, plants and animals, life and death, and unity of the earth. The tales are intended for reading aloud and are followed by ideas for discussion and science teach-

ing activities. The activities focus on sensory awareness of the earth, understanding the earth, caring for the earth, or caring for people.

★Carew, Jan. (1974). *The third gift*. Illustrated by Leo & Diane Dillon. Boston: Little, Brown (out of print). [African]
The Jubas are led by the prophet Amakosa to the foot of Nameless Mountain. Here each new leader climbs the mountain to bring the clan a gift. The tribe receives work, beauty, and imagination from the consecutive leaders. In telling the story, Jan Carew demonstrates the gift of language with figurative expressions. The abundance of idioms and metaphor makes this a book to be read aloud with a discussion of the picturesque language.

Carpenter, Frances. (1949). *Tales of a Chinese grandmother*. Illustrated by Maithe Hasselriis. New York: Doubleday. [Chinese]
The grandmother of the Ling household is introduced in the first chapter. Each following chapter is a tale she tells her grandchildren. Conclusions concerning Chinese culture can be drawn from these stories. It offers a good model for collecting and recording folklore.

Carpenter, Frances. (1947, 1987). *Tales of a Korean grandmother*. Rutland, VT: Tuttle College. [Korean]
Thirty-two short stories are adapted from many sources with an imaginative mixture of genuine folktales, cultural facts, and storyteller's fantasy. The fairy tales and legends are told in the setting of a Korean family, with wise Grandmother Kim telling the grandchildren the stories. This folktale collection, which continues to be reprinted in both Japan and the United States, is available in paperback.

★Carrick, Carol. (1989). *Aladdin and the wonderful lamp*. Illustrated by Donald Carrick. New York: Scholastic. [Arabian]
This artistically retold, simplified story from the *Arabian Nights* brings this tale to the eight- to ten-year-old reader with dramatic, vivid illustrations set in the Middle East. The main omissions are the flying carpet, the intrigue of the sorcerer, and developing the character of Aladdin as a well-loved, generous, and coura-

geous leader. The story is well suited for reader's theater or dramatizing.

*Cauley, Lorinda B. (1988). *The pancake boy.* New York: Putnam. [Norwegian]

> Mother Goody Poody makes pancakes for her seven hungry children, and a large, round pancake escapes the pan and rolls out of the house. He is chased by Goodman Poody, seven squally children, Manny Panny, Henny Penny, Cocky Locky, Ducky Lucky, Goosey Poosey, and eaten by Piggy Wiggy. Action-packed illustrations encourage the child to retell the story, following the predictable, repetitive pattern. It is very similar to "Gingerbread Boy." The book includes a Norwegian recipe for sweet-milk pancakes.

Chase, Richard. (1973). *Grandfather tales.* Boston: Houghton Mifflin. [Regional American]

> Tales commonly known through European collections appear here with the local color and dialect of the Appalachian settler. Compare the language and story line in these tales with other familiar versions. "The Old Sow and Three Shoats" is similar to "Three Pigs," "Ashpet" resembles "Cinderella," and "Sody Sallyraytus" is like "Three Billy Goats Gruff."

Chase, Richard. (1943). *The Jack tales.* Illustrated by Berkeley Williams, Jr. Boston: Houghton Mifflin. [Regional American]

> These stories from southern Appalachia with the style and humor of mountain folk are variants of English tales. Jack is a human hero who has fantastic adventures and always wins. Familiar themes include "Jack and the Bean Tree" and "Jack and the North West Wind." Draw conclusions about the character from the action of the story.

*Climo, Shirley. (1989). *The Egyptian Cinderella.* Illustrated by Ruth Heller. New York: Crowell. [Egyptian]

> The tale of Rhodopis (ra-doh-pes), recorded in the first century B.C., is one of the oldest Cinderella stories. It is based on a historical fact that a Greek slave girl, Rhodopis, married the Phar-

aoh Amasis in the twenty-sixth Dynasty, 570–526 B.C. Rhodopis received a pair of rose-red slippers from her master as a reward for her beautiful dancing. This caused even more ill treatment from the Egyptian servant girls, and she was left home when all the girls went to the Pharaoh's court. A falcon picked up one of the rose-red slippers and dropped it on the Pharaoh's lap. This began the search for the maiden who could wear the slipper and become his wife. Ruth Heller's colorful paintings bring the reader into a stylized Egypt of the Pharoahs.

*Coatsworth, Emerson, & Coatsworth, D. (1980). *The adventures of Nanabush: Ojibway Indian*. New York: Atheneum (out of print). [Native American]

These legends concern Nanabush, a powerful Manitou, or spirit, of the Ojibway world. He is both a provider and a trickster. Tales tell how and why things are as they are today as a result of either Nanabush's creativeness or his trickery. Each tale is a model of the unique blending of the components of a legend, as handed down by the Canadian Indians. The preface gives interesting information about the collectors of the tales and the Indian illustrator.

*Cole, Joanna. (1989). *Anna Banana: 101 jump-rope rhymes*. Illustrated by Alan Tiegreen. New York: Morrow. [Regional American]

This book is included as representative of the traditional rhymes and songs that are passed down from generation to generation of children at play. The rhymes are divided by the various types of jump-rope games Joanna Cole found the children playing. The subjects generally relate to everyday living. Some traditional rhymes reflect political views of the day. Sources at the end of this book will interest the pupil who would like to find other such collections.

*Conover, Chris. (1986). *Froggie went a-courting*. New York: Farrar, Straus & Giroux. [English]

The illustrator sets this familiar nursery rhyme in Elizabethan England, with the small animals assuming the culture and dress of the eighteenth century style. Meanwhile, a peasant girl is picking berries from a bush, clearly depicting the contrast between real life and the tiny magical kingdom. The pictures offer art lessons for students of all ages.

*Conover, Chris. (1989). *Simple Simon*. New York: Farrar, Straus & Giroux. [English]

The illustrations are the basis for including this book of an individual nursery rhyme in this guide. Each page includes in the background scenes other nursery characters and illustrations of action in nursery rhymes. For example, three small pictures show the story of Jack and Jill getting water, Jack falling, and Jill tumbling after. The hidden stories offer a delightful way for retelling the rhymes with knowledgeable young children.

*Corrin, Sara & Stephen. (1988). *The Pied Piper of Hamelin*. Illustrated by Errol LeCain. New York: Harcourt Brace Jovanovich. [German]

Three strikingly illustrated versions of the Pied Piper have been published since the 700th anniversary at Hamelin of the loss of 130 of its children on June 26, 1284. Whatever the truth of the historical dark day, this legend has persisted and was introduced to English-speaking children in Browning's poem "The Pied Pier of Hamelin." The Corrin version is action-filled, offering descriptive visual pictures of the happenings in the village for the listener. The artwork provides medieval designs and expressive, compelling illustration of the village people and events. Compare with other versions of the same tale.

Courlander, Harold, & Hertzog, G. (1988). *The cow-tail switch and other West African stories*. Illustrated by MadyeLee Chastain. New York: Holt, Rinehart & Winston. [African]

Many of the African tales in this collection are remarkable for their play-on-words humor. Characters are given names that relate to the action of the story; one man is named Time and another called Nothing.

*Crouch, Marcus. (1989). *Ivan: Stories of old Russia*. Illustrated by Bob Dewar. Oxford, England: Oxford University Press. [Russian]

Ivan is the fool of Russia. He is the butt of jokes, the youngest son, the lazy one—but also cunning and resourceful. This volume from the Oxford Myth and Legend series contains sixteen stories about Ivan. The reader is introduced to Baba Yaga, the witch that all Russian children know. In some stories Ivan is a prince, in others he is a peasant, but he always ends up in favor. The characters can be compared among the stories with similar characters from other countries.

D'Aulaire, Ingri & Edgar. (1965). *Book of Greek myths.* New York: Doubleday. [Greek]

This timeless resource book begins with a classic illustration of the family of Zeus. Stories include the major gods and goddesses, the minor gods, and the mortal descendants of Zeus. The language evokes imagery, and the stories are generally short and full of action. Compare the storytelling style with Virginia Hamilton's *In the Beginning.* A study of the Greek gods should also include *The Olympians,* an informational book about the gods and goddesses by Leonard Fisher (1984). This collection is particularly suitable for middle-school study.

*Delacre, Lulu, selector. (1989) *Arroz con leche: Popular songs and rhymes from Latin America.* Translated by Elena Paz. New York: Scholastic. [Latin American]

Traditional songs, games, and rhymes were selected to give a cross-section of children's folklore from Argentina, Mexico, and Puerto Rico. Directions are given for playing the group games, and musical arrangements by Ana-Maria Rosado are included. Soft pastel illustrations offer pleasing images of the countries and children represented. This collection can offer sparkle to a social studies unit and inspire collecting folklore.

*Demi. (1987). *The hallowed horse.* New York: Dodd, Mead. [Indian, Asian]

In Indian legend the first kings possessed supernatural powers, which they in turn gave to mortal counterparts. A young king gets his magic in a hallowed horse who helps him conquer Kaliya, the multiheaded snake. The reader is introduced to the pomp and splendour of ancient India and the royal astrologers. The artistry and mood of the story are told through the delicate illustrations that include Indian symbols.

★Demi. (1980). *Liang and the magic paintbrush*. New York: Holt, Rinehart & Winston. [Chinese]

A poor boy who longs to paint is given a magical paintbrush by a man who appears on a phoenix. Liang's gift brings joy to the common people, but devastation for the greedy emperor. The richly detailed watercolor offers a fine example of Chinese art.

★dePaola, Tomie. (1978). *The clown of God*. New York: Harcourt Brace Jovanovich. [Italian]

This Renaissance tale gives the modern reader a picture, both by word and illustration, of the society of old Italy. This version of the legend of the little juggler giving his talent to the Christ Child is well suited for pantomime or creative dramatics.

★dePaola, Tomie. (1981). *Fin M'Coul: The giant of Knockmany Hill*. New York: Holiday House. [Irish]

This story takes an episode from the life of the popular Irish folklore giant. His wife is the true heroine, and she saves Fin from another giant by trickery. The illustrations and rhythmical dialogue make this version an entertaining delight for children of all ages. *Fin M'Coul* is a good choice for creative dramatics or pantomime.

★dePaola, Tomie. (1980). *The Lady of Guadaloupe,* or *Nuestra Senora de Guadalupe*. New York: Holiday House. [Mexican]

dePaola retells the legend of the appearance of the Virgin Mary to a poor farmer in Mexico in 1531. Since this edition is also printed in Spanish, the tale is a good choice for the bilingual classroom or in a unit about Mexico.

★dePaola, Tomie. (1983). *Legend of the Bluebonnet*. New York: Putnam. [Native American]

A Comanche Indian legend tells of the origin of the wild lupine, nicknamed "Bluebonnet" by Texan settlers. The shaman, or medicine man, has told the tribe that the drought and famine they are suffering is caused by the people becoming selfish and taking from the earth without return. A little girl gives her precious doll with blue feathers to the Great Spirits. In return the

Spirits fill the meadow with blue flowers and the rains begin to fall. An excellent story for reader's theater or creative drama.

*dePaola, Tomie. (1980). *The legend of Old Befana*. New York: Harcourt, Brace. [Italian]

On the Feast of the Three Kings, January 6, Old Befana visits the children of Italy in her perennial search for the Christ Child. In retelling the tale dePaola researched the artistic symbols as well as the legend sources. His version of the old woman who answers the invitation too late to find her way to Bethlehem portrays her as a kindly, lonely person rather than a witch. Compare Old Befana with the Russian Babushka. The version of *Babushka* described in this guide is by Charles Mikolaycak.

*dePaola, Tomie. (1975). *Strega Nona*. Englewood Cliffs, NJ: Prentice-Hall. [Italian]

Strega Nona and her magical pasta pot is a favorite folktale for young children. Big Anthony's dilemma can be depicted in dramatic play. With repeated readings, the children join in on the pasta pot rhymes. Tomie dePaola's illustrations resemble stage settings and provide ideas for making stage scenery.

*dePaola, Tomie. (1986). *Tomie dePaola's favorite nursery tales*. New York: Putnam. [International]

This collection includes traditional tales and fables that should be part of all young children's literary background. The retelling is clear, true to tradition, and rhythmical in use of predictable phrases and repetitions. The illustrations help develop concepts of size and number as well as offer entertaining caricatures of familiar folk and animals. It fulfills a basic need in a preschool, kindergarten, or first-grade library.

*DeRoin, Nancy. (1975). *Jataka tales: Fables from the Buddha*. Illustrated by Ellen Lanyon. Boston: Houghton Mifflin. [East Indian]

These thirty fables were originally told by the Buddha 500 years before Christ, according to legend. Similarities to Aesop's fables are apparent: Animals speak and act, life situations require basic decisions, and the solutions are stated with morals. Differences appear in the underlying philosophy. The Jataka tales point to solutions to problems through recognizing the importance of the individual and the need to accept and understand realities of life. Aesop fables point to attempts to manipulate external forces and control or overcome enemies. Comparisons of the fables will enhance a study of theme with intermediate-grade children.

*Esbensen, Barbara. (1989). *Ladder to the sky.* Illustrated by H. K. Davie. Boston: Little, Brown. [Native American]
     This Ojibway legend tells how illness and death came to the people and how it was followed by the gift of healing plants. The flowing, rich language and lovely, colorful paintings dramatize the close relationship of the people with the earth. The illustrator's research on Ojibway customs, clothing, and medicinal plants is beautifully incorporated into the borders and the pictures. The book would fit well with the teaching ideas in *Keepers of the Earth* by Michael Caduto and Joseph Bruchac.

*Esbensen, Barbara. (1988). *The star maiden.* Illustrated by H. Davie. Boston: Little, Brown. [Native American]
     This transformation tale is a retelling of a version written by an Ojibway chief, George Copway, in 1850. A star tires of wandering in the sky and stops near the camp of the Ojibway Indians. She appears in the dream of a young brave and asks if she can live with them. The people welcome her, and after trying other forms of life, she finds her place as a water lily. Each soft, lovely painting in the book is framed with beautiful patterns from Ojibway sources.

Finger, Charles. (1924). *Tales from silver lands.* Illustrated by Paul Honore. New York: Doubleday. [South American]
     Finger relates the origins of many of the tales that he records. This is the most extensive collection of authentic South American tales available at present. "The Tale of the Gentle Folk" is a good one to read to the class as an example of how folktales were believed by the natives. One story that deals directly with the results of making judgments based on inadequate information is "The Tale That Cost a Dollar."

*Freedman, Florence. (1985). *Brothers: A Hebrew legend.* Illustrated by Robert A. Parker. New York: Harper & Row. [Hebrew]

This remarkable legend of brotherly love should be read aloud to audiences of all ages. Each brother shows concern for the other when a drought causes a shortage of food. The parallel actions of the brothers, the simple language, and delicate drawings contribute to the concluding song, "How good it is for brothers to live together in friendship."

★Gackenbach, Dick. (1977). *The leatherman.* New York: Seabury Press. [Regional American]

The mood is set for this intriguing tale with an opening description of Ben's dream, in which a leather coat floats "like a ship from a fog" and Ben is "drowning in an ocean of molasses." Vivid word imagery characterizes this real-life tale based on the travels of the eccentric Jules Bourelay, the leatherman, who wandered the countryside of Connecticut in the mid-1880s. The line-and-wash drawings capture the feelings of the boy when he confronts the strange man.

Gag, Wanda. (1979). *The sorcerer's apprentice.* Illustrated by Margot Tomes. New York: Coward, McCann. [European]

The boy becomes an apprentice to the evil sorcerer under the pretense of being illiterate. In secret, he reads the sorcerer's books of spells and tricks. The good apprentice is able to win over the bad sorcerer, proving that sorcery can be used for good as well as evil. The exemplary plot with an easily recognized theme, a quick introduction, suspense, logical development, and swift conclusion is a good model for writing.

★Galdone, Paul. (1975). *Billy goats gruff.* New York: Seabury Press. [Norwegian]

This version of the "Billy Goats Gruff" story pictures a very mean troll that alternately delights and frightens the young listener. Creative dramatic play, with the children providing their own words and actions, is an entertaining way to get preschoolers and kindergartners responding to literature.

★Galdone, Paul. (1975). *The gingerbread boy.* New York: Seabury Press. [Regional American]

Galdone retells the classic nursery tale in clear, easy-to-read, and literary style. The repetition of the gingerbread boy's chant, and the account of the many folk who run after him, make this a story that the beginning reader can soon read alone. The comical illustrations help tell the story and jog the reader's memory if a word or phrase is forgotten.

★Galdone, Paul. (1968). *Henny-Penny.* New York: Seabury Press. [English]

Henny-Penny is a cumulative animal tale. The repetition makes it a favorite with beginning readers. Other versions of this story are titled "Chicken Licken" or "Chicken Little." The plot and sequence of the story can be extended by having the young reader draw the animals, cut them out, and manipulate them in retelling the story.

★Ginsburg, Mirra. (1988). *The Chinese mirror: A Korean folktale.* Illustrated by M. Zemach. New York: Harcourt Brace Jovanovich. [Korean]

A humorous story of the first time the people in a small Korean village ever saw a mirror. First the villager, then his wife, next his mother-in-law, his father-in-law, their young son, and finally a neighbor each see a different stranger looking at them. The dramatic illustrations add to the humor and to seeing the cultural old Korean community.

Ginsburg, Mirra. (1973). *The lazies: Tales of the peoples of Russia.* New York: Macmillan. [Russian]

This collection of tales is based on the theme that indolence will bring no reward. The humorous tales include much of folk wisdom and humor. By focusing on the variety of ways the theme is presented, the reader can be directed to an evaluation of plot structure.

Ginsburg, Mirra. (1973). *One trick too many.* Illustrated by Helen Siegl. New York: Dial. [Russian]

The trickster animal of Russia is the fox, and his tales are beautifully told by Mirra Ginsburg as collected and translated from her own childhood in Russia. At times the fox knows when to stop his tricks, but at other times his cleverness gets him into trouble. This collection contains stories that fit each of the subgroups of animal tales. The woodcuts, printed in yellow, red, and black, depict scenes from the tales framed with symbolic animal and plant forms.

Ginsburg, Mirra. (1975). *Three rolls and one doughnut.* Illustrated by Anita Lobel. New York: Dial. [Russian]
    The varied characters and the way their problems are amusingly resolved in the legends, fables, and riddles of this collection depict Russian people as part of the universal heritage of folk culture and as persons with humor and wisdom. These stories were collected and translated from Mirra Ginsburg's childhood in Russia. Her concise direct style provides easy reading.

★Goble, Paul. (1984). *Buffalo Woman.* New York: Macmillan. [Native American]
    The buffalo was a source of life for the Plains Indians. This tale varied from tribe to tribe, but it was always used to teach that the buffalo and the people were related. The intent was to strengthen the bond with the herds and to encourage the buffalo to give of himself for the people. Goble's highly stylized drawings portray the power and force of the buffalo and picture the close bond between buffalo and Indian. Discussion of this book with intermediate-grade children can help develop an understanding of Indian culture.

★Goble, Paul. (1988). *Her seven brothers.* New York: Bradbury. [Native American]
    The designs of the Indian clothing and painted tepees in this book are based on Cheyenne patterns, as found in museums in the United States and Europe. This legend tells the story of the Big Dipper. A young Cheyenne girl had the gift of speaking with and understanding the spirits of all things. She sewed seven beautiful sets of clothing, which she brought to seven brothers who lived far into the north land. She lived with the seven brothers until one day the Buffalo People came for her. The final flight for their lives sent them into the sky, where they still live today.

★Goble, Paul. (1989). *Iktomi and the berries.* New York: Watts. [Native American]

Goble presents the lore of the Plains Indians to young readers through simple, funny tales of the trickster Iktomi, or Spider. Sometimes Iktomi uses his cleverness to help humans, while at other times he offers mischief or foolishness. Children learn what is unacceptable from Iktomi's terrible behavior without undue moralizing. In this humorous story of prideful Iktomi, Goble offers storytelling suggestions for the adult reader. *Iktomi and the Boulder,* published by Watts in 1988, explains why there are rocks scattered through the Great Plains and why bats have flattened faces.

*Goble, Paul. (1983). *Star boy.* Scarsdale, New York: Bradbury. [Native American]

Goble's exquisite, brilliant drawings combine with clear, literary language to make this version of "Star Boy" (Scarface) a fascinating story of the Sky World. Within the story, which is worthy of enjoying on its own merit, one also learns why the Blackfeet dance the Sun Dance, a ceremonial thanksgiving to their Creator. Legendary information about the Evening and Morning Star is given. *Star Boy* provides background information that enhances the reading of SanSouci's *The Legend of Scarface.*

*Goode, Diane. (1989). *The Diane Goode book of American folk tales & songs.* Collected by Ann Durell. New York: Dutton. [Regional American]

The stories and songs come from a variety of regions and ethnic groups, including a Native American trickster tale, a version of "Knee-High Man," and a Davy Crockett story. Notes of the melody are written for songs such as "Buffalo Girl," "I've Been Working on the Railroad," "Billy Boy," and "Clementine." The lively language and humorous illustrations offer good entertainment for listening to and looking at oral history.

Graham, Gail. (1970). *The beggar in the blanket & other Vietnamese tales.* Illustrated by Brigitte Bryan. New York: Dial. [Vietnamese]

The main character in each fairy tale in this collection is a strong woman, and the theme concerns overcoming her subservient role in society. Whether a princess or a peasant, she is able to assert herself through character traits of determination, wisdom, courage, and intrigue. Not all the characters are perfect, and some of the tales end in tragedy. Gail Graham translated the stories from French sources found in Saigon libraries.

*Grifalconi, Ann. (1986). *A village of round and square houses.* Boston: Little, Brown. [African]
> The village of Tos really exists on the side of a volcano in the Cameroons of Central Africa. Through the voice of a young woman who grew up there, the story is told of why all the men live in square houses and all the women live in round houses. The expressive, full-color paintings offer a dynamic picture of the village and the gentle people who live there. The rhythmic, flowing language makes this an excellent read-aloud book. The superb, dramatic art won a Caldecott Honor medal.

*Grimm, Jacob & Wilhem. (1981). *Cinderella.* Illustrated by Nonny Hogrogian. New York: Greenwillow. [German]
> This version of Cinderella uses a hazel tree, planted by Cinderella, and a white dove as tools of enchantment rather than a fairy godmother and a pumpkin. Lovely, powerful artwork enhances the tale. Compare with other European versions as well as the Chinese and Vietnamese stories. See Perrault, Louie, and Vuong entries in this guide.

*Grimm, Jacob & Wilhelm. (1980). *The fisherman and his wife.* Translated by Randall Jarrell and illustrated by Margot Zemach. New York: Farrar, Straus & Giroux. [German]
> Picturesque language and an abundance of conversation characterize this charming version of a familiar folktale. The greedy woman and the simple fisherman are pictured in their changing environment with both humor and imagination. This is a good story for children to illustrate from their own visual images before Zemach's drawings are shared. The vivid description of the sea is worthy of note.

*Grimm, Jacob & Wilhelm. (1990). *The frog prince.* Retold by Jan Ormerod and David Lloyd. Illustrated by Jan Ormerod. New York: Lothrop, Lee & Shepard. [German]
> This version of the tale of enchantment and love matches the

quality of storytelling in the Grimms' *Princess and the Frog* retold by Rachel Isadora and offers an expressive, poetic text with delicate, fairylike paintings. The phrase "my honey, my heart" recurs in lyrics sung by the frog to the princess. Comparing the text with the illustrations will develop appreciation for beautiful art and language.

*Grimm, J. & W. (1980). *Hansel and Gretel*. Illustrated by Susan Jeffers. New York: Dial Press. [German]

The soft, pastel illustrations mute the harshness of the story of two children abandoned by their father and stepmother. Hansel and Gretel appear to be in charge of the situation, and the witch is portrayed as a humorous rather than a scary creature. The reader gets the impression that all will turn out well, in true fairy tale style. Contrast this with the Grimm story retold and illustrated by Lizbeth Zwerger (1979). Her misty, brown-toned background projects an eerie feeling, and Hansel and Gretel sit forlornly outside the cottage. Her grotesque witch meets mixed response from the readers. I recommend that this comparison be made with children from eight to eleven years of age rather than younger children.

*Grimm, Jacob & Wilhelm. (1989). *Princess and the frog*. Retold and illustrated by Rachel Isadora. New York: Macmillan. [German]

The colorful watercolor illustrations capture the pomp and ceremony of this palace tale. The princess breaks the enchantment when she keeps her promise. The frog must sleep with a princess for three nights before he can change back into a man. The beauty of the artwork and the sprightly, rhymical text combine to offer an exemplary version of this tale from the castle.

*Grimm, Jacob & Wilhelm. (1974). *Snow White*. Translated by Paul Heins and illustrated by Trina Hyman. Boston: Little, Brown. [German]

For the child who has heard only the Walt Disney version of "Snow White," this story will be a surprise. The oral tradition of the story and the translation based on the early written version should be explained to the listener or child reader. The reader should be at least eight years old if he or she is to understand the

fantasy of this story. The illustrations portray a dark and foreboding German forest, realistically interpreting the setting of the
tale.

★Grimm, Jacob & Wilhelm. (1972). *Snow White and the seven dwarfs.*
Translated by Randall Jarrell and illustrated by Nancy Burkert. New
York: Farrar, Straus & Giroux. [German]
    The text, as translated by Randall Jarrell, is similar to the trans-
    lation by Paul Heins (immediately above). The main difference is
    in the illustration. Nancy Burkert's forest and dwarfs are less
    foreboding than those of Trina Hyman. The kingdom appears as
    a magical, mythical world. A discussion about the feelings that
    different illustrations evoke helps readers recognize the contri-
    bution the pictures make to the mood of the story.

★Hague, Kathleen. (1980). *East of the sun and west of the moon.* Illustrated by Michael Hague. New York: Harcourt Brace Jovanovich.
[Norwegian]
    This complex story was a favorite of the girls in a sixth-grade
    class. It includes many characteristics of a classical fairy tale: a
    broken promise, supernatural feats, a quest. All this is accom-
    plished by a girl who wins the prince rather than a boy who wins
    the princess. Mystical illustrations extend the story. Compare
    with fairy tales from China, Russia, or Africa, noting how the
    distinctiveness of the setting influences the elements of the story.

★Haley, Gail. (1970). *A story, a story.* New York: Atheneum. [African]
    Ananse wants the Sky-God's stories and succeeds in accomplish-
    ing the three feats required to win the treasure. This version can
    be read by a child with limited ability because of the predictable
    style and repetition. Compare with the Native American legend
    of how stories came into the world in *Keepers of the Earth* by
    Michael Caduto and Joseph Bruchac.

★Hamilton, Virginia. (1987). *In the beginning.* Illustrated by Barry
Moser. New York: Harcourt Brace Jovanovich. [International]
    This excellent collection of twenty-five creation stories from
    around the world is enhanced by the brief, informative com-
    ments following each tale. The myths, retold with clarity and

beauty, tell about the origin of the universe, gods, our planet, and the creation of humankind. Myths from each continent and a number of countries are included. Moser's imaginative, bold artwork sets a tone of grandeur and awe for the people's beliefs.

*Hamilton, Virginia. (1985). *The people could fly: American black folktales*. Illustrated by Leo & Diane Dillon. New York: Knopf. [Regional American]

This volume offers a major contribution to American folk literature and to understanding the African American history of slavery. The theme of enduring the tyranny of man is expressed with incredible humor and pathos in each type of tale. Animal tales depict a variety of common animals taking on the characteristics of people within the plantation environment, with the slaves identifying with the clever small rabbit. The fairy tales, including both exaggerated and supernatural tales, show the underdog as the hero, overcoming difficulties through impossible means. Tales of freedom are moving stories with reality narrative interwoven with folktale motifs such as talking animals or a magic hoe.

Harris, Christie. (1977). *Mouse Woman and the mischief makers*. Illustrated by Douglas Tait. New York: Atheneum (out of print). [Native American]

As a supernatural being called Narnauk, Mouse Woman guarded the seas and wilderness of Canada's northwest coast. Anyone disturbing the order of this part of the world was a mischief maker, and Mouse Woman would deal with him! Most of the tales are concerned with humans desiring what they should not have and misusing natural resources. The stories end with some variant of "No good ever comes of upsetting the proper order of the world." Provides a good introduction to a study of ecology.

Harris, Christie. (1976). *Mouse Woman and the vanished princess*. Illustrated by Douglas Tait. New York: Atheneum (out of print). [Native American]

The library card summary labels these stories legends. However, the reader will find many characteristics of fairy tales in the adventures of the Indian princesses who are carried away by supernatural forces and rescued through great adventures, each one assisted by Mouse Woman.

Harris, Christie. (1973). *Once more upon a totem*. Illustrated by Douglas Tait. New York: Atheneum (out of print). [Native American]
    The artform of the symbolic totem comes alive in the expressive imagery of Harris in telling three celebrated stories from the potlatch feasts. The use of figurative language captures the mystery of nature that permeates the Indian beliefs. A discussion of "The People Who Owned the Stories" is a fitting culmination to the study of folk literature.

Harris, Christie. (1963). *Once upon a totem*. Illustrated by John Frazer Mills. New York: Atheneum (out of print). [Native American]
    A totem pole was usually raised to honor a particular chief, living or dead. The story behind each crest tells how one of the symbols came to be the emblem of a mythical ancestor. "The One Horned Mountain Goat" is the same story told by Toye in *The Mountain Goats of Temlaham*. Compare the different storytellers' use of language.

Harris, Joel Chandler. (1955). *The complete tales of Uncle Remus*. Compiled by Richard Chase and illustrated by Arthur Frost. Boston: Houghton Mifflin. [African American]
    The stories of Br'er Rabbit as told by Joel Harris are written in dialect that needs much practice before it can be read to a group. The dialogue and unusual expressions make a fascinating word study for an individual project. All of the tales were collected from African Americans. Harris made a conscientious attempt to reproduce the way the slaves talked in his area of the South. The social setting of his tales depicts Uncle Remus, the black slave, telling the story to a little white boy, the son of the plantation owner. A comparison of this collection with the retelling by Julius Lester shows a very different voice of the narrator.

Hayes, Joe. (1986). *The day it snowed tortillas*. Illustrated by Lucy Jelinek. Sante Fe, NM: Mariposa Publishing. [Mexican American]
    The ten *cuentos*, stories told to entertain, are ones told throughout the Hispanic villages in New Mexico. They probably originated

in Spain and traveled north from Mexico as conquistadores and colonists moved north. The collection includes cautionary tales that teach morals through the antics of wise and foolish heros. Stories with motifs similar to European tales are "Little Gold Star," a Cinderella story, "LaLlorona," a ghost story, and "The Prince," a typical fairy tale. The stories are an entertaining mixture of recognizable motifs and Hispanic customs and humor.

*Hinajosa, Francisco. (1984). *The old lady who ate people.* Illustrated by Leonel Maciel. Boston: Little, Brown. [Mexican]
These tales were collected by listening to people in the countryside and from anthropological collections. These are stories from the native Indians, not the Spanish settlers. The distinctive illustrations offer an example of the authentic, vigorous style of the Indians of Guerrero, a state in Mexico. The stories reflect the violent and strange powers of the gods, but good wins against evil. The stories are "The Wise Woman of Cordoba," "The Voice of the Dead," "The Chantal Giant," and "The Old Lady Who Ate People."

*Hodges, Margaret. (1989). *The arrow and the lamp: The story of Psyche.* Illustrated by D. Diamond. Boston: Little, Brown. [Greek]
In Greek mythology, Psyche is human, the daughter of a king and queen who becomes a goddess after she performs all the feats required of her by Aphrodite, the goddess of love and beauty. Aphrodite is jealous of Psyche's beauty and sends Eros, god of love, down to wound her with his arrows and find her a mean-tempered husband. Instead, Eros falls in love with her. Aphrodite sets obstacles in the way of her marriage to Eros. Psyche's adventures parallel those of the maiden in the Norwegian tale *East of the Sun and West of the Moon* (see Hague). The illustrations complement this classic Greek myth with delicate, interpretive artistry.

*Hodges, Margaret. (1972). *The fire bringer.* Illustrated by Peter Parnall. Boston: Little, Brown. [Native American]
The Paiute Indians tell how Boy was told by Coyote that with the help of a hundred swift runners they could get fire to keep people warm and help them cook their food. The runners form

a relay to pass the fire from Burning Mountain to their caves. The Indians' questions concerning fire demonstrate the need to suspend judgment. The reader learns how difficult it is to understand an idea without background.

★Hodges, Margaret. (1984). *Saint George and the dragon*. Illustrated by Trina Schart Hyman. Boston: Little, Brown. [English]
Caldecott Medal–winning illustrations present a stunning picture of the English medieval countryside. Hodges retells a segment of a legend immortalized in Spenser's *The Faerie Queen*. George slays the dreadful dragon and brings peace to the land. This is an excellent choice for puppetry, drama, or reader's theater.

★Hodges, Margaret. (1964). *The wave*. Illustrated by Blair Lent. New York: Houghton Mifflin. [Japanese]
This classic Japanese folktale is retold for children with rich language and a clear, suspense-filled plot. The wise old man who lives on top of the mountain sees a tidal wave coming to destroy the village below. He and his six-year-old grandson set fire to his rice fields to get the people to come up the mountain. He saves the lives of 400 villagers. Blair Lent's whirling illustrations made with cardboard cutouts capture the feel of the sea and the danger to the village.

★Hogrogian, Nonny. (1971). *One fine day*. New York: Macmillan. [Armenian]
This is a cumulative nursery tale in which the fox makes a number of bargains before getting his tail back from the old woman. Young children can chant the refrain, draw pictures in sequence, or improvise a presentation of this story.

★Hooks, William H. (1987). *Moss gown*. Illustrated by Donald Carrick. New York: Clarion Books. [Regional American]
This southern traditional Cinderella tale includes elements of King Lear, perhaps from the English storytellers who settled in the tidewaters of eastern North Carolina. Candace has been driven from her home by a father who misunderstands her, and a witch woman gives her a gossamer moss gown that becomes beautiful when a chant is recited. Candace hides the gown when

she becomes a mistreated kitchen girl and remembers it when three balls are planned at the mansion. In the end, she is reunited with her father. A similar tale is told by Appalachian tellers, with a gown of rushes rather than moss.

*Hooks, William H. (1989). *The three pigs and the fox.* Illustrated by S. D. Schindler. New York. Macmillan. [Regional American]
    The story of the three pigs came to Appalachia with the early English, Scots, and Irish settlers more than three centuries ago. Many years of storytelling have added local color and regional language. This literary version is based on several oral versions heard in the Smoky Mountain area. The pigs leave, one by one, to make their own way in the world and are told by mama to remember three things. Pig three, Hamlet, rescues his brothers from mean, tricky old drooly-mouth fox and fulfills mama's orders. The story should be read for enjoyment of the picturesque, rhythmical language, and expressive illustrations.

*Hou-tien, Chieng. (1980). *Six Chinese brothers: An ancient tale.* New York: Holt, Rinehart. [Chinese]
    The strength of the Chinese family is portrayed by six sons, each using their supernatural physical power to save first their father's life, and then their brothers' lives. They win the favor of the king. In contrast to the ethnic demeaning implied in Clair Bishop's (1938) version illustrated by Kurt Wiese, this version, with the delicate scissor-cut illustrations by a Chinese artist, reflects appreciation of Chinese culture.

*Huck, Charlotte. (1989). *Princess Furball.* Illustrated by Anita Lobel. New York: Greenwillow. [English]
    This version of Cinderella depicts a spunky princess who uses her own ingenuity to overcome her unhappy life. The king promises his motherless daughter in marriage to an ogre (the hated marriage motif). When she could not dissuade him, she asks for three bridal dresses and a coat made of a thousand kinds of fur. To her amazement he produces the gifts, so she runs away dressed in the fur coat. A young king finds this mysterious furball in the hollow of a tree. She works as a servant in his castle, but wears the gowns to the balls, and wins the respect and love

of the king. Compare with *Tattercoats* by Flora Steele, another English Cinderella, and with versions from other countries.

*Hutton, Warwick. (1989). *Theseus and the minotaur.* New York: Macmillan. [Greek]

This classic Greek myth relates the heroic deeds of the son of the king of Athens, who rescues the city's young men and women from death by the Minotaur, monster son of the king of Crete. However, Theseus abandons Ariadne and forgets to change the boat's black sail to white, thus leading to his father's death. Hutton's clear, vibrant narrative and brilliant, expressive illustrations make this story understandable to intermediate-grade children. The heroism thwarted by misjudgment offers opportunity for guiding critical thinking and stimulating discussion. It should be compared to other versions, because Hutton omits the appearance of the god Dionysus, who forbids Theseus to marry Ariadne.

*Ishii, Momoko. (1987). *The tongue-cut sparrow.* Translated by Katherine Paterson and illustrated by S. Akaba. New York: Dutton. [Japanese].

This is a Japanese variation on the theme of a kind old man and a greedy wife. The characters and behaviors of the couple are clearly contrasted in descriptions and in the unfolding of the story. The translation includes onomatopoeic words from the Japanese language to add pleasure to reading the tale aloud. Pronunciation and explanations for the Japanese words are given in the back of the book. Compare to the German *The Fisherman and His Wife* by the Grimm brothers.

Jaffrey, Madhur. (1985). *Seasons of splendour: Tales, myths and legends of India.* New York: Atheneum. [Indian, Asian]

Many stories from the rich heritage of India are in print for the first time in this collection. Jaffrey arranged the tales in the sequence of a Hindu calendar year, since each story is traditionally told on the moon-day. The stories are prefaced with an explanation of their influence on her childhood in India. A pronunciation guide offers valuable help for reading the stories aloud. Hearing these stories would make an important contribution to a cultural study of the Indian people.

Jagendorf, Moritz. (1968). *Ghostly folktales.* Illustrated by Oscar Liebman. Morristown, NJ: Silver Burdett. [International]
Ghost stories from many places in the world make intriguing reading for Halloween. "The Tale of the Hairy Toe" and "The Coffinmaker's Ghost Party" were favorites of many sixth-graders in one class. The students made posters with the message of their favorite scary story for Halloween.

*Johnston, Tony. (1990) *The badger and the magic fan.* Illustrated by Tomie de Paola. New York: Putnam. [Japanese]
Principal folktale characters in Japan are the *tengu* goblin children, who carry fans, have large red noses, and represent pride. In this story, the *tengu* have a magic fan that can make a nose longer or shorter. The Japanese trickster, the badger, covets the fan and changes himself into a little girl. He begins his trickery, first with the *tengu* to get the fan, then with a very rich girl, and finally with the rich man, winning his daughter in marriage. The *tengu* find their fan, and the story ends its comical plot with the biggest trick of all against the badger. The stylized illustrations add to the charm and humor of the book. The *tengu* are depicted as mischievous rather than proud.

Kimmel, Eric A. (1988). *Anansi and the moss-covered rock.* Illustrated by Janet Stevens. New York: Holiday House. [African]
This is a story of one of Anansi's tricks. He used a magical moss-covered rock to trick other animals out of their carefully collected food until Bush Deer turns the trick back on Anansi. The predictability of the story and the rhythmical, repetitive language makes this an appealing story to use with young children. See Figure 3.4 for a story staircase model of this tale used with kindergarteners.

*Laird, Elizabeth. (1987). *The road to Bethlehem.* New York: Collins & Sons. [Ethiopian, African]
This book is not catalogued as folk literature because the story is not an exact translation of the manuscript text. However, it is

worthy of inclusion here because it weaves Ethiopian legends from before Christ into the Christmas narrative as believed by the folk. The illustrations are reproduced from eighteenth-century handpainted manuscripts commissioned by kings and queens of Ethiopia, currently owned by the British Museum. Archbishop Terry Waite, Great Britain, writes in the foreword, "I hope this book will increase compassion and enlarge respect for a people who can be justly proud of their traditions."

Leach, Maria. (1982). *Whistle in the graveyard. Folktales to chill your bones.* Illustrated by Kenn Rinciari. New York: Macmillan. [International]

> From all over the world traditional tales about ghosts are collected here and classified by the types of ghosts. The introduction gives background; notes and bibliography at the end give sources and motifs. The very short stories capture the interest of the reluctant reader.

Lee, Jeanne. (1985). *Toad is the uncle of heaven.* New York: Holt, Rinehart & Winston. [Vietnamese]

> This pourquoi tale explains why the toad has become a symbol of rain in Vietnam. A devasting drought causes the toad to go to see the King of Heaven. Along the way, he collects several animals to go with him, and they save his life with their special abilities. A good story to use as a model pourquoi or for predicting what will happen next.

★LeGalliene, Eva. (1982). *Legend of the Milky Way.* New York: Holt, Rinehart & Winston. [Chinese]

> The first written version of this tale appeared in the *Book of Odes,* collected by Confucius in the fifth century B.C. The queen mother of the heavens separates the heavenly weaver princess from her earth husband, the flute player, by making them into stars. On the seventh day of the seventh month of the Chinese year, the princess, now the star Vega, goes across the silver river to visit her husband, Altair. A map of the constellations at the back of the book can stimulate the reader to learn more about stories behind the stars. Use with *Keepers of the Earth* by Michael

Caduto and Joseph Bruchac and *They Dance in the Sky: Native American Star Myths* by Jean Monroe and Ray A. Williamson.

*Lester, Julius. (1989). *How many spots does a leopard have?* Illustrated by David Shannon. New York: Scholastic. [African and Jewish]
   Fairy tales, animal tales, and legends make up this lively collection of ten African and two Jewish stories. Julius Lester emphasizes the universality of the tale, and yet the distinctiveness of the culture comes through clearly. End notes describe the differences between his translation and the original stories and give the sources and area of the country from which they came. The stories are full of rhythmical language and bright imagery. Drawings offer a mood of suspense and drama, as well as humor.

Lester, Julius. (1972). *The knee-high man and other tales.* Illustrated by Ralph Pinto. New York: Dial. [African American]
   Six animal stories from American slave lore include trickster tales of Mr. Rabbit and Mr. Bear, familiar characters in black folktales, and the pourquoi tale "Why Waves Have Whitecaps." This is a good collection to read aloud for demonstrating the distinctiveness of animal tales, and to distinguish between the trickster tale, the pourquoi tale, and the fable.

*Lester, Julius. (1987). *Tales of Uncle Remus: The adventures of Brer Rabbit* (Volume I). Illustrated by Jerry Pinkney. New York: Dial.

*Lester, Julius. (1988). *More tales of Uncle Remus: Further adventures of Brer Rabbit, his friends, enemies, and others* (Volume II). Illustrated by Jerry Pinkney. New York: Dial. [African American]
   In these two volumes, a total of eighty-five Brer Rabbit tales are retold in the language of African Americans, "where sound is as important as meaning" (Vol. I, p. x). In the foreword, Lester describes how he writes the tales using the voice of Uncle Remus and explains the role of the Uncle Remus character in Joel Harris's collections. The tales are arranged in the books by themes. Occasional introductory paragraphs explain the connection of one tale to another. The teller does not change the story line of these authentic tales but does make contemporary references, which he describes as characteristic of black storytelling. Inter-

mediate-grade children can compare this collection with the Joel Harris collection. Reading parts of the introductions in either volume to a group of readers would offer a lively discussion on the role of the storyteller and where the stories begin.

*Lewis, Richard. (1988). *In the night, still dark.* Illustrated by Ed Young. New York: Atheneum. [Hawaiian]

Poetry from the folk offers the reader a sense of the feelings of people toward important events in their lives. This sensitively illustrated poem is an adaptation from the *Kumulipo,* a traditional Hawaiian creation chant. It can be classified with myths, since it was chanted over a newborn child to help bond the new life to all other living things. The poem also portrays the Hawaiians' concept of evolution and the emergence of daylight. It can be enjoyed for its simple rhythms and for the beautiful expressions in both the language and the shapes and forms of the vivid artwork.

*Louie, Ai-Ling. (1982). *Yeh Shen.* Illustrated by Ed Young. New York: Philomel Books. [Chinese]

This version of Cinderella is translated as it appeared in the *Miscellaneous Record of Yu Yang,* a book that dates from the T'ang dynasty (618–907 A.D.). The oldest European version of Cinderella is an Italian tale, published in 1634. Young's lovely artwork repeats the fish motif on nearly every page, providing picturesque foreshadowing of the plot. A comparison of the Chinese Cinderella with the European one will show marked similarities and differences in the two versions.

*Lund, Janet, & Laszlo, Gal. *The twelve dancing princesses.* Toronto: Methuen. [German]

This is a fairy tale of a simple farm boy who follows his dream, obeys the three commands of an old woman, and solves the mystery of twelve princesses who wear out a pair of dancing shoes each night. The artwork presents lovely panoramas of the imagined countryside. Lund's clear retelling offers an appealing story to be read aloud for enjoyment and as an example of a model fairy tale.

\*Mahy, Margaret. (1990). *The seven Chinese brothers.* Illustrated by Jean and Mou-sien Tseng. New York: Scholastic. [Chinese]
This version of the story of brothers with magical traits is based on translation from folktales collected at the time of Emperor Ch'in Shih Huang in 259–210 B.C. The tale follows classic tall tale tradition in the accounts of each man innocently using his powerful attribute. In the end, the wicked, demanding emperor dies in a brother's flood of tears and the brothers become heroes for the suffering builders of the Great Wall of China. The richly detailed illustrations are as carefully researched as the text.

\*Manson, Christopher. (1989). *A gift for the king.* New York: Henry Holt. [Arabian, Iranian]
This legend from the fourth century B.C. is a simple story of a discontented king who leaves his palace for a walk in his kingdom and is pleased by a gift from a small child. The extravagance of the palace and the absolute rule of the Persian monarch are clearly evident in the actions and speeches of the people. The richly detailed illustrations help young readers recognize the opulence of the ancient empire. Manson used preserved palace wall carvings and historical constructions of costumes, furniture, and buildings as sources for his paintings.

\*Mayer, Marianna. (1985). *Aladdin and the enchanted lamp.* Illustrated by Gerald McDermott. New York; Macmillan. [Arabian]
The *Arabian Nights* (or *Thousand and One Nights*) originates from three distinct cultures: Persian, Indian, and Arab. It appeared in an Arabic edition about 850 A.D. The earliest manuscript that included the Aladdin tale was found in Baghdad in 1703. It has been translated into many languages. The elegant, vivid language and spectacular paintings in this version lure readers into the Middle East and the adventures of Aladdin. Aladdin wins over the wicked sorcerer, using the magic lamp, a golden ring, flying carpets, and the powerful genie wisely. Recommended for grades 5–8.

\*Mayer, Marianna. (1987). *Beauty and the beast.* Illustrated by Mercer Mayer. New York: Macmillan. [French]
The theme of this romantic English fairy tale is the strength and

beauty of enduring love. Beauty agrees to live with the beast in order to save her father from death and her family from poverty. She grows to love the beast, which frees him from the enchantment of the wicked fairy and transforms him back into a prince. The imaginative, lively paintings interpret the fanciful, romantic mood of the story. Compare it with the Norwegian *East of the Sun and West of the Moon* by Kathleen Hague, in which the beast is less frightening but the task of the merchant's daughter is more difficult. Also compare it with the French version retold and illustrated by Jan Brett (1990), who pictures the beast as a wild boar.

★Mayer, Marianna. (1989). *The twelve dancing princesses*. Illustrated by K. Y. Craft. New York: Morrow. [German]

Rich, expressive language and exquisite artwork combine to offer the reader a romantic, enchanting tale. This elegant retelling leaves the reader with a sense of the depth of the magical spell and the relief of the royal family when the princesses are returned to normal. The beauty of the language makes this a story that should be read aloud to all ages. Intermediate-grade children should be given time to study and delight in the delicate, jewel-like paintings and artistic form of the book.

★McDermott, Beverly Brodsky. (1976). *The Golem: A Jewish legend*. Philadelphia: Lippincott (out of print). [Jewish]

Brilliant gouache, watercolor, dye, and ink drawings enhance this fine version of the legend recalled from the Jewish ghetto of Prague, Czechoslovakia. Recommended for critical discussion with older children (ages nine through twelve). The quotation that prefaces the book can direct the attention of the listeners and invoke a discussion of beliefs. This legend presents the idea that man cannot be like God. Whatever man creates can never match God's creation.

★McDermott, Gerald. (1977). *Anansi the spider*. New York: Holt, Rinehart & Winston. [African]

This story is typical of the multidimensional African folktales that reveal universal beliefs and parallel tales from other countries. Anansi goes on a long journey and is saved from disaster by his sons, each of whom uses his special ability as suggested by his name: See Trouble, Road Builder, River Drinker, Game Skinner, Stone Thrower, and Cushion. Compare with *The Riddle of the Drum,* by Verna Aardema, and *Six Chinese Brothers,* by Chieng Hou-tien.

*McDermott, Gerald. (1974). *Arrow to the sun.* New York: Viking. [Native American]

This Pueblo Indian myth is analogous to the Bible story of Christ's birth. Mocked by others because Boy doesn't know his father, Boy sets out on a search that leads to the Sun Lord. He passes through four chambers of ceremony to prove his birthright. Colorful, symbolic graphic designs are intriguing to intermediate-grade children.

*McDermott, Gerald. (1975). *The Stonecutter.* New York: Viking. [Japanese]

Tasaku becomes discontented as a lowly stonecutter, and the spirit of the mountain grants his wish to become a prince. As further discontent leads to further wishes, Tasaku comes to understand, too late, the value of his position as stonecutter. McDermott (1975) made a film of this legend before writing the book. A comparison of the film and the book can lead to a discussion by intermediate-grade children about what each medium contributes to the emotional impact of the message, and to an understanding of the theme.

*McDermott, Gerald. (1980). *Sunflight.* New York: Four Winds Press. [Greek]

McDermott provides an authentic, though abbreviated, interpretation of the myth of Daedalus and Icarus. Daedalus, the master craftsman, engineers the escape of himself and his son, Icarus, from the wicked king, Minos. However, the escape ends in tragedy because Icarus does not obey his father. If a basal reader used in your class contains an abridged version of this legend, read McDermott's version to the students for a comparison. The colorful symbolic illustrations help to interpret the mood of the story and add dignity to the narration.

*McVitty, Walter. (1988). *Ali Baba and the forty thieves*. Illustrated by Margaret Early. New York: Abrams. [Arabian]

The drama and suspense of this popular tale from *The Arabian Nights* make it very appealing to the ten- to twelve-year-old reader. This version is an excellent retelling with a stately style that fits the grandeur of the tale and with a liveliness that makes it understandable to the young reader. The elegant illustrations are done in the style of authentic Persian miniatures, with decorative borders in brilliant colors and gold. The text could be adapted by the children for reader's theater or for an operetta script.

*Mikolaycak, Charles. (1984). *Babushka: An old Russian folktale*. New York: Holiday House. [Russian]

This traditional legend tells the story of an old lady who declines an invitation to meet the Christ Child. She spends the rest of her life searching for him and leaving gifts for children all over the world. The brilliantly painted illustrations show the changing seasons, the passing of years, and different countries that she visits. The artwork offers a striking example of how pictures enrich and enlarge a story.

*Milnes, Gerald. (1990). *Granny will your dog bite and other mountain rhymes*. Illustrated by K. Root. New York: Knopf. [Regional American]

Milnes collects rhymes, ditties, verses, and riddles from his West Virginia mountain neighbors and presents here a lively, authentic Appalachian volume of verse. An introductory author's note offers interesting information about his collecting. The rhymes must be read aloud and the contagious rhythms will have the children joining in with delight. The illustrations provide a humorous, lively, warm portrait of the area and its people.

Monroe, Jean G., & Williamson, Ray A. (1987). *They dance in the sky: Native American star myths*. Illustrated by Edgar Stewart. Boston: Houghton Mifflin. [Native American]

Native Americans have told tales of the origin of the stars throughout generations. An astronomer and a teacher/writer collaborate in this book to present an outstanding collection of star myths. Stories and beliefs of various Native American tribes are written in a clear style for intermediate readers. The glossary, index, and bibliographies offer further information for a study of Native American Indians.

*Moore, Marianne. (1954). *The fables of La Fontaine*. New York: Viking (out of print). [European]
    La Fontaine's fables are based on Aesop's collection. The delicate illustrations add to their appeal and interpretation. The use of conversation makes these versions appealing to the reader and appropriate for dramatizing.

*Mosel, Arlene. (1968). *Tikki tikki tembo*. Illustrated by Blair Lent. New York: Holt, Rinehart & Winston. [Chinese]
    The Chinese have given all their children short names ever since the near tragedy of this "first and honored" son Tikki tikki tembo-no sa rembo-chari bari ruchi-pip peri pembo. Finely drawn illustrations add humor to this excellent version of a favorite legend. Elements of this story fit well into the definition of legend.

*Morimoto, Junko. (1986). *The inch boy*. New York: Viking. [Japanese]
    The Japanese counterpart to Tom Thumb begins with an old couple praying to Buddha for a child. A baby one-inch long arrives at their doorstep. They name him Issunboshi. His determination to become a Samurai brings him to Kyoto, where he has many adventures. His destruction of the Red Demon ends with his touching the Demon's magic hammer and growing to full size. The compelling illustrations by the author combine cartoonlike caricatures with expressive backgrounds of Japanese landscape.

Norman, Howard. (1989). *How Glooskap outwits the ice giants*. Illustrated by M. McCurdy. Boston: Little, Brown. [Native American]
    These six entertaining stories tell how the giant mythical creator, Glooskap, prepared the world for human beings and how he worked hard protecting his people from forces of evil and natural disaster. The final story tells how he turned himself into an In-

dian and found a home in a secret, peaceful place in his creation. The wood engravings capture the mystery, humor, and drama of the stories. The rich language used by Norman offers visual images that would stimulate the listener or reader to illustrate the dramatic events in the stories.

*Otsuka, Yuzo. (1981). *Suho and the white horse.* Illustrated by Sue-kichi Akaba. New York: Viking. [Mongolian]

This legend is retold with beautiful literary language that captures the feelings of the boy and his love for the beautiful horse. After grieving, Suho conquers his sorrow and makes a new kind of musical instrument from the bones of the horse, as he was commanded in a dream. The mood-setting watercolor illustrations help the reader picture the wide expanse of the desolate Mongolian countryside. The reading of this legend could be accompanied by music simulating the sound of the Mongolian horsehead fiddle.

*Perrault, Charles. (1976). *Cinderella, or the little glass slipper.* Illustrated by Erol LeCain. Harmondsworth, England: Puffin. [French]

This French version of Cinderella has stylistic, ethereal illustrations. It includes a fairy godmother as the source of enchantment, with the transformed pumpkin and mice for the coach and horses. The discerning reader will enjoy a comparison of both illustrations and text with versions from other countries; see *Cinderella* by the Grimms and *Yeh Shen* by Ai-Ling Louie. See also two other versions of the French Cinderella (Perrault, 1985, 1988). Over 300 versions of Cinderella have been recorded.

*Ransome, Arthur. (1968). *The fool of the world and the flying ship.* Illustrated by Uri Shulevitz. New York: Farrar, Straus & Giroux. [Russian]

Fool is kind to an old man. The old man changes his poor food into a feast and gives Fool instructions for finding a supernatural flying machine. Fool follows his advice to the letter and flies over the countryside, picking up people he meets. Each of his passengers possesses special gifts that help Fool perform feats necessary to win the czar's daughter. The theme, that God loves simple folk and turns things to their advantage in the end, is found in many Russian tales.

\*SanSouci, Robert. (1978). *The legend of Scarface*. Illustrated by Dan SanSouci. New York: Doubleday. [Native American]

Scarface is ridiculed by his peers for his appearance and his poverty. He undertakes an adventurous trip to the sun and is successful because of his kindness to all he encounters. Read to the class as an example of how a legend unfolds. This story also gives enough information to allow the reader to draw conclusions through a predictable plot. *Star Boy*, retold by Paul Goble, provides background for this episode.

\*SanSouci, Robert. (1989). *The talking eggs: A folktale from the American South*. Illustrated by Jerry Pinkney. New York: Dial. [Regional American]

Creole culture is richly expressed in both the text and the detailed illustrations. This cautionary tale tells about a good sister, a bad sister, and a greedy mama who receive what they deserve from an old woman. The cautionary theme of good being rewarded and evil punished is told with surprising and entertaining variants. This is an excellent story to read aloud to a small group so that all could enjoy the illustrations along with the reading.

Schwartz, Alvin. Schwartz's books make a significant contribution to American folklore. All are products of careful collecting, using extensive research and reliable source documentation. In his collections of folklore, sayings, and traditions, he described people's ideas, hopes, and dreams. His books not only offer interesting folklore information, but also are models for children to use in collecting lore. This is a representative list of his books. There are many others, including easy-to-read books:

(1974). *Cross your fingers, spit in your hat: Superstitions and other beliefs*. Illustrated by Glen Rounds. New York: Lippincott.

(1980). *Flapdoodle: Pure nonsense from American folklore*. Illustrated by John O'Brien. New York: Harper & Row.

(1988). *Gold and silver, silver, and gold: Tales of hidden treasure*. Illustrated by David Christiana. New York: Farrar, Straus & Giroux.

(1981). *Scary stories to tell in the dark: Collected from American folklore.* Illustrated by Stephen Gammell. New York: Lippincott.

(1985). *Tales of trickery from the land of spoof.* Illustrated by David Christiana. New York: Farrar, Straus & Giroux.

(1987). *Telling fortunes: Love magic, dream signs, and other ways to learn the future.* Illustrated by Tracey Cameron. New York: Lippincott.

(1972). *A twister of twists, a tangle of tongues.* Illustrated by Glen Rounds. New York: Harper & Row.

(1975). *Whoppers: Tall tales and other lies collected from American folklore.* Illustrated by Glen Rounds. New York: Harper & Row.

(1973). *Witcracks: Jokes and jests from American folklore.* Illustrated by Glen Rounds. New York: Harper & Row.

★Silverman, Maida. (1984). *Anna and the seven swans.* Illustrated by David Small. New York: Morrow. [Russian]

This story appeals to young children and is a less scary introduction to Baba Yaga than other tales cited in this guide. The lively illustrations help verify the magic in the tale. Anna is able to save her brother because Baba Yaga is helpless in the presence of love and caring.

★Singer, Isaac Bashevis. (1967). *Mazel and Shlimazel or the milk of the lioness.* Illustrated by Margot Zemach. New York: Farrar, Straus & Giroux. [Jewish]

This is a Russian folktale concerned with the war between good and evil. Mazel would bring happiness to the poorest of the village for one year, then Shlimazel would try to undo what Mazel had done in one second. The story is characterized by superb use of language and an intriguing weaving of the plot. The plot structure will help the reader make judgments about the good and evil forces in the story.

Singer, Isaac Bashevis. (1968). *When Shlemiel went to Warsaw and other stories.* New York: Dell. [Jewish]

"Shrewd Todie and Lyser the Miser," "The Elders of Chelm and Genendel's Key," and "When Shlemiel Went to Warsaw" are stories in this collection that deal with amiable fools who convince the town wise men that their actions are logical. In addition to enjoying the stories for their humor and the Russian regard for the foolish man, Singer's use of figurative language and imagery offers examples to use in verifying understanding of figurative language.

★Small, Ernest. (1966). *Baba Yaga*. Illustrated by Blair Lent. Boston: Houghton Mifflin. [Russian]

The character of Baba Yaga is developed in this story about Marusia, who is captured by Baba Yaga, and a hedgehog who is really a boy who has been enchanted by the black sunflower that Baba Yaga is seeking. Baba Yaga is portrayed as a horrible but basically harmless witch who is easily influenced but hard to escape from completely. This caricature of Baba Yaga should be compared with other authors' renditions for comparisons of the way the witch is portrayed.

★Sneve, Virginia Driving Hawk. (1989). *Dancing teepees: Poems of American Indian youth*. Illustrated by Stephen Gammell. New York: Holiday House. [Native American]

This collection highlights stories, chants, songs, and prayers told by generation after generation to Native American children. It includes works of contemporary tribal poets who write of traditional events in the lives of the Native American children. Gammell's symbolic drawings give the appearance of being drawn on animal hides and parchment with natural dyes. Sneve dedicates the book "to the memory of my grandmothers whose stories showed me the power of the oral tradition and who taught me to love words."

★Steele, Flora. (1976). *Tattercoats*. Illustrated by Diane Goode. New York: Bradbury Press (out of print). [English]

Unfortunately, this lovely Cinderella story is out of print but perhaps can be found in a library. The grandfather, a lord, spends his lifetime mourning the death of his daughter and refusing to see her child. She grows up with no one caring for her, and her only friend is a goatherd. He becomes the source of magic, and she wins the love of the prince because of her beauty before her gown is changed at the ball. The watercolor illustrations, painted on parchment, expressively interpret the tale.

*Steptoe, John. (1987). *Mufaro's beautiful daughters*. New York: Lothrop, Lee & Shepard. [African]

Steptoe's modern folktale is included in this collection of traditional tales because it so truly captures the essence of an African tale written in Theal's collection, *Kaffir Folktales,* published in 1895. The illustrations were inspired by an ancient city in Zimbabwe, and the characters' names are from the Shona language. The beauty and dignity of the story give an image of worthy, considerate rulers and caring villagers. The motifs of pride brought low and modesty rewarded offer comparison with European and Oriental Cinderella tales. The transformation motif takes the form of the prince changing himself into a hungry boy, an old woman, and Nyoka, a snake, for testing the two daughters.

*Stevens, Janet. (1987). *The town mouse and the country mouse*. New York: Holiday House. [European]

The familiar fable of the mouse cousins is told in contemporary language and contemporary drawings. Conversations between the two emphasize the extreme contrast between their values. The illustrations emphasize the difference between the two environments. The artist offers fascinating views from the perspective of the mice, who on some pages are drawn nearly lifesize. The fable ends with the moral, "It's better to have beans and bacon in peace than cakes and pies in fear."

Stoutenberg, Adrien. (1968). *American tall tale animals*. Illustrated by Glen Rounds. New York: Viking. [Regional American]

The names of the "strange animals lolloping around in the early days of our country" arouse the curiosity of the reader of these fantastic stories collected from throughout the United States. The colloquialisms of the various regions and the picturesque language can be appreciated by the discerning reader.

Timpanelli, Gioia. (1984). *Tales from the roof of the world: Folktales of Tibet*. Illustrated by Elizabeth Lockwood. New York: Viking. [Tibetan]

Four unusual tales give the reader a sense of an exotic, fascinating country. Each story ends with "And the sun of happiness shone on the mountaintop, and the staff of misery was washed away in the river." The gifted reader will be intrigued with the mystical mood of the Tibetan stories and the wise feminine characters. The humor and drama in the tales make them good choices for storytelling. Symbols of the Buddhist religion are pictured and explained at the end of the book.

*Tolstoy, Alexei. (1968). *The great big enormous turnip*. Illustrated by Helen Oxenbury. London: Heinemann. [Russian]
This simple cumulative tale tells of the need for teamwork. Everyone from grandpa to the mouse is needed to pull up the turnip. The message and the story patterns make this book an excellent choice for dramatic play, chanting, and sequence pictures.

*Towle, Faith. (1975). *The magic cooking pot*. Boston: Houghton Mifflin. [Indian, Asian]
This version of a favorite Indian folktale is illustrated with batik. The illustrations are made with the traditional Indian colors— yellow, orange, red, maroon, and black. The story is about a poor religious man who is given two magic cooking pots from the goddess Durga and his adventures with the pots. It can be used for a study of art or a character study.

*Toye, William. (1988). *How summer came to Canada*. Illustrated by Elizabeth Cleaver. New York: Walck. [Native American]
When Indians were created, Winter moved from his Far North home into Eastern Canada. Glooskap, creator of the Indians, goes south to find Queen Summer, captures her, and returns to his country. Summer overcomes Winter and suggests a compromise. The rich, glowing colors of Elizabeth Cleaver's collage illustrations enhance the mood of the seasonal setting. This legend is recommended for reading to the class as an introduction to the importance of setting.

*Toye, William. (1977). *The loon's necklace*. Illustrated by Elizabeth Cleaver. Toronto: Oxford University Press. [Native American]
This is a Canadian legend of a blind man whose sight is restored by the loon who leads him into the lake. The man throws his

shell necklace to the bird, and the beads become the white markings on the black loon feathers. Compare with "The Blind Boy and the Loon," retold by Ramona Maher (1969), and with the film *The Loon's Necklace* (1981). In the film version the man saves the whole tribe from starving, not just his family, and the shell necklace is more than a prized belonging, holding meaning as a medicine man's tradition.

★Toye, William. (1988). *The mountain goats of Temlaham*. Illustrated by Elizabeth Cleaver. New York: Walck. [Native American]
This legend is beautifully illustrated with brilliant collage displaying Indian designs and totems. The law of the hunt from old times was to kill only what was needed for meat and skin and antlers. The legend deals with the consequences of disregarding the law. Characters are revealed through action and description, with little dialogue. The difference in the amount of information given about a character and the need for drawing conclusions is demonstrated through a comparison with the same tale told by Ramona Maher (1969).

★Troughton, Joanna. (1986). *How the birds changed their feathers*. New York: Bedrick Books. [South American]
Many South American Indian tribes share this pourquoi tale from the days when all birds had white feathers. It includes a transformation motif, with a boy turning into a rainbow snake. The excuses each animal makes to keep from hunting the snake add humor to the tale and offer a model for children writing their own pourquoi stories.

★Vinci, Leonardo da. (1973). *Fables of Leonardo da Vinci*. Collected by Bruno Nardini and illustrated by Adriana S. Mazza. Northbrook, IL: Hubbard Press (out of print). [European]
Nardini collected these from Leonardo da Vinci's manuscripts. Nardini attributed their origin to Leonardo, although in the past five centuries, tales in this collection have circulated through storytellers in Italy and France. The message of the fables is universal and fits today's society as well as the ancients. Fine drawings complement the tales.

⋆Vuong, Lynette. (1982). *The brocaded slipper and other Vietnamese tales*. Illustrated by Vo-Dinh Mai. Reading, MA: Addison-Wesley. [Vietnamese]

> Counterparts to the familiar European fairy tales are translated in this carefully documented collection. Tam, in "The Brocaded Slipper," is a Cinderella character. Little Finger, in "Little Finger of the Watermelon Patch," shares characteristics of Thumbelina. Tu Thuc, in "The Fairy Grotto," reminds the reader of Rip Van Winkle. "Master Frog" had to work much harder than the frog prince to gain his real identity. Quynh, an Eastern fairy princess, is similar to the Goose Girl. A comparison of these Vietnamese tales and their Western counterparts demonstrates the unique individuality of each culture and also the bonds of common humanity.

⋆Willard, Nancy. (1989). *East of the sun and west of the moon*. Illustrated by Barry Moser. New York: Harcourt Brace Jovanovich. [Norwegian]

> Nancy Willard retells the classic fairy tale in play form, featuring players, off-stage voices, and puppets. She recommends a simple set and minimal scenery. The story of the brave girl who travels through magical lands to rescue the prince from being wed to a troll is told poetically. The first scene is a conversation among the four winds and sets the stage for interpreting the story. When the girl breaks her promise to the bear and lights the candle her mother gave her, the scene is told by the East Wind and mimed by the characters. Act III tells the dramatic, brave journey of the girl to find the prince and rescue him from the captive marriage to the hideous daughter of the Troll Queen. This would make an excellent reader's theater production.

⋆Williams-Ellis, A. (1987). *Tales from the enchanted world*. Illustrated by Moira Kemp. Boston: Little, Brown. [International]

> These stories were chosen by Lady Amabell Williams-Ellis to help children increase their understanding of countries other than their own and were first published in England. The tales are written for storytelling with advisory notes and information about other variations. Her lively writing style features sprightly conversations and well-translated rhymes and chants. Stories are told

from Russia, Tibet, Africa, the West Indies, China, Norway, Ireland, Germany, and England. Dramatic full-color paintings and striking black line drawings enrich the enchanted mood.

*Yagawa, Sumiko. (1981). *The crane wife*. Translated from Japanese by Katherine Paterson and illustrated by Suekichi Akaba. New York: Morrow. [Japanese]

Poetical, classical language marks this version of the ancient transformation tale. When Yohei breaks his word to his beautiful, mysterious wife, he loses her forever. The illustrations follow a traditional technique of Japanese painting in which various shades of water-thinned ink are laid on paper with soft brush strokes in delicate shadings. This most-loved folktale has been made into plays, movies, and an opera in Japan.

*Yep, Laurence. (1989). *The rainbow people*. Illustrated by David Wiesner. New York: Harper & Row. [Chinese American]

Yep collected tales from Chinese who came to California in the mid-nineteenth century from Kwangtung. His explanatory notes offer a wealth of personal, historical information for understanding the cultural, political, and economic influence on the shaping of the stories. The magic in the tales is exciting and mysterious. The tales are divided by topics: "Tricksters," "Fools," "Virtues and Vices," "In Chinese America," and "Love." The intriguing tales and the interesting notes offer a rich mosaic of Chinese American culture.

Yolen, Jane, editor. (1986). *Favorite folktales from around the world*. New York: Pantheon. [International]

In her introduction, Jane Yolen states that enjoyment of folktales requires "only a listening ear and an open heart." She has chosen a wide variety of tales from forty different cultures and has organized them into thirteen sections by type (trickster, wonder tales) or theme (age and infancy, fooling the devil). Each section is introduced with background material, and end notes provide sources and further explanations, providing information for study. Many of the stories are ones she has heard from storytellers.

★Yolen, Jane. (1986). *The sleeping beauty.* Illustrated by Ruth Sander-son. New York: Knopf. [English]

> This exquisite rendition captures the romantic aura and beauty of the familiar fairy tale through both poetic prose and artwork. At the christening of the promised princess, the curse of the thir-teenth fairy is softened by the twelfth fairy, who changes the death by spindle prick to a hundred-year sleep. On her fifteenth birthday Briar Rose finds the fateful spinning wheel. The search of the prince is told with suspense-filled action. The vivid illus-trations were first painted in oil on stretched canvas. Sanderson received inspiration from English pre-Raphaelite artists and drew the characters from models dressed in costume.

★Young, Ed. (1989). *Lon Po Po: A Red-Riding Hood story from China.* New York: Philomel. [Chinese]

> The tale of Granny Wolf comes from ancient oral tradition of northern China. Three daughters are home alone while their mother goes to visit their granny. The wolf comes disguised as their grandmother, Po Po, and he blows out the candle when he enters the house. Shang, the oldest and most clever daughter, does not trust the thorny hands and hairy face. She escapes to gather gingko nuts to feed him, taking her sisters with her, and plots the fate of the the wolf. The clever daughters outsmart the wolf. The dramatic art, which captures the mood of the girls and the action of the tale, won the Caldecott award.

★Zelinsky, Paul O. (1986). *Rumpelstiltskin.* New York: Dutton. [Ger-man]

> This version of the German fairy tale is based on an early version of the story and brings to life the splendor of the medieval set-ting. The rich oil paintings are reproduced so colorfully that the reader wants to touch the gold to see if it is real. Text and illus-tration collaborate in presenting a vivid portrait of the characters. The little man who helps the princess (miller's daughter) in her dilemma is a loveable elf. This rendition offers a tale to be enjoyed by all ages, not only primary-grade children.

★Zemach, Harve. (1986). *Duffy and the devil.* Illustrated by Margot Zemach. New York: Farrar, Straus & Giroux. [English]

This is a Cornish tale, similar to "Rumpelstiltskin," in which a devil agrees to help Duffy, a lazy and clumsy hired girl, do her spinning and knitting for three years. A mixture of original Old Cornish dialect with modern English highlights the text as the old housekeeper helps Duffy by luring the squire to the devil's hideaway. The illustrations contribute effectively to the character portrayal.

*Zemach, Harve. (1977). *Salt: A Russian tale*. Illustrated by Margot Zemach. Chicago: Follett. [Russian]
   This traditional tale tells of a merchant with three sons who seek their fortune with their father's ships. The youngest foolish brother is the hero of the tale. Folktale motif D1601 appears here as a magic mill continuously making salt. Compare it to the magic pasta pot in *Strega Nona* as told by Tomie dePaola. The amusing figures of speech and rich use of language make the story a delight to read.

*Zemach, Margot. (1977). *It could always be worse: A Yiddish folktale*. New York: Farrar, Straus & Giroux. [Jewish]
   A poor man is crowded in his house with mother, wife, and six children. He follows the advice of the rabbi, and his problems go from bad to worse. Finally his life returns to what it was at the beginning, and he is contented. An excellent predictable tale to read to beginning readers. The humorous illustrations show the life of the peasants and their silly situations.

*Zvorykin, Boris, & Onassis, Jacqueline. (1978). *The firebird*. New York: Viking. [Russian]
   Zvorkyin presented this exquisitely illustrated volume of Russian tales to France in gratitude for his new life there. The English translation followed classic versions of the tales. The high adventure of Prince Ivan in search of a firebird would be a good choice for modeling the artistry of story along with ballet music. The stories offer an excellent combination of a distinctively Russian setting and a universal plot in quest tales.

# Appendix A

## FOLK LITERATURE BY REGION AND CULTURE

The books contained in A Guide to Recommended Folk Literature for Children are listed here by geographic region and, in the case of Euro-Asian cultures, by the specific cultural group wherein the tale originated.

### Africa

Aardema, Verna. *Bringing the Rain to Kapiti Plain*
    *Who's in Rabbit's House?*
    *Why Mosquitoes Buzz in People's Ears*
Bernstein, Margery, & Kobrin, Janet. *The First Morning: An African Myth*
Bryan, Ashley. *Lion and the Ostrich Chicks*
    *The Ox of the Wonderful Horns and Other African Tales*
Carew, Jan. *The Third Gift*
Climo, Shirley. *The Egyptian Cinderella* (Egypt)
Courlander, Harold, & Hertzog, G. *The Cow-Tail Switch and Other West African Stories*
Grifalconi, Ann. *A Village of Round and Square Houses*
Haley, Gail. *A Story, a Story*
Kimmel, Eric. A. *Anansi and the Moss-covered Rock*
Laird, Elizabeth. *The Road to Bethlehem* (Ethiopia)
Lester, Julius. *How Many Spots Does a Leopard Have?*
McDermott, Gerald. *Anansi the Spider*
Steptoe, John. *Mufaro's Beautiful Daughters*

## American Continents

**NATIVE AMERICAN**

Baker, Olaf. *Where the Buffaloes Begin*

Baylor, Byrd. *A God on Every Mountain Top*
     *And It Is Still That Way*

Bernstein, Margery, & Kobrin, Janet. *The Summer Maker: an Ojibway Indian Myth*

Bierhorst, John. *The Girl Who Married a Ghost and Other Tales from The North American Indian*
     *The Naked Bear: Folktales of the Iroquois*
     *The Ring in the Prairie*

Caduto, Michael, & Bruchac, Joseph. *Keepers of the Earth*

Coatsworth, Emerson, & Coatsworth, D. *The Adventures of Nanabush: Ojibway Indian*

dePaola, Tomie. *Legend of the Bluebonnet*

Esbensen, Barbara. *Ladder to the Sky*
     *The Star Maiden*

Goble, Paul. *Buffalo Woman*
     *Her Seven Brothers*
     *Iktomi and the Berries*
     *Star Boy*

Harris, Christie. *Mouse Woman and the Mischief Makers*
     *Mouse Woman and the Vanished Princess*
     *Once More Upon a Totem*
     *Once Upon a Totem*

Hodges, Margaret. *The Fire Bringer*

McDermott, Gerald. *Arrow to the Sun*

Monroe, Jean G., & Williamson, Ray A. *They Dance in the Sky: Native American Star Myths*

Norman, Howard. *How Glooskap Outwits the Ice Giants*

SanSouci, Robert. *The Legend of Scarface*

Sneve, Virginia Driving Hawk. *Dancing Teepees: Poems of American Indian Youth*

Toye, William. *How Summer Came to Canada*
     *The Loon's Necklace*
     *The Mountain Goats of Temlaham*

**HAWAIIAN**
Lewis, Richard. *In the Night, Still Dark*


**REGIONAL AMERICAN**
Bang, Molly Garrett. *Wiley and the Hairy Man*
Chase, Richard. *Grandfather Tales*
     *The Jack Tales*
Cole, Joanna. *Anna Banana: 101 Jump-Rope Rhymes*
Gackenbach, Dick. *The Leatherman*
Galdone, Paul. *The Gingerbread Boy*
Goode, Diane. *The Diane Goode Book of American Folk Tales & Songs*
Hamilton, Virginia. *The People Could Fly: American Black Folktales*
Harris, Joel Chandler. *The Complete Tales of Uncle Remus*
Hooks, William. *Moss Gown*
     *The Three Pigs and the Fox*
Lester, Julius. *The Knee-High Man and Other Tales*
     *Tales of Uncle Remus: The Adventures of Brer Rabbit*
     *More Tales of Uncle Remus: Further Adventures of Brer Rabbit, His
          Friends, Enemies, and Others*
Milnes, Gerald. *Granny Will Your Dog Bite and Other Mountain
     Rhymes*
SanSouci, Robert. *The Talking Eggs: A Folktale from the American
     South*
Schwartz, Alvin. See A Guide to Recommended Folk Literature for
     Children for specific titles
Stoutenberg, Adrien. *American Tall Tale Animals*
Yep, Laurence. *The Rainbow People*


**MEXICAN**
Aardema, Verna. *The Riddle of the Drum: A Tale from Tizapan, Mexico*
Bierhorst, John. *Spirit Child*
Blackmore, Vivien. *Why Corn Is Golden: Stories about Plants*
dePaola, Tomie. *The Lady of Guadaloupe,* or *Nuestra Senora de Gua-
     dalupe*
Hayes, Joe. *The Day It Snowed Tortillas*     (Mexican–American)
Hinajosa, Francisco. *The Old Lady Who Ate People*

**CENTRAL, SOUTH AMERICAN, WEST INDIES**
Bryan, Ashley. *The Dancing Granny*
      *Turtle Knows Your Name*
Delacre, Lulu. *Arroz con leche: Popular Songs and Rhymes from Latin America*
Finger, Charles. *Tales from Silver Lands*
Troughton, Joanna. *How the Birds Changed their Feathers*

## Western European

Aesop. *Aesop's Fables*. Illustrated by Michael Hague
      *Aesop's Fables*. Illustrated by Heidi Holder
      *Aesop's Fables*. Illustrated by Lisbeth Zwerger
Gag, Wanda. *The Sorcerer's Apprentice*
Moore, Marianne. *The Fables of La Fontaine*
Stevens, Janet. *The Town Mouse and the Country Mouse*
Vinci, Leonardo da. *Fables of Leonardo da Vinci*

**ENGLISH**
Conover, Chris. *Froggie Went A-Courting*
Conover, Chris. *Simple Simon*
Galdone, Paul. *Henny-Penny*
Hodges, Margaret. *Saint George and the Dragon*
Huck, Charlotte. *Princess Furball*
Steele, Flora. *Tattercoats*
Yolen, Jane. *The Sleeping Beauty*
Zemach, Harve. *Duffy and the Devil*

**FRENCH**
Brown, Marcia. *Stone Soup*
Mayer, Marianna. *Beauty and The Beast*
Perrault, Charles. *Cinderella, or the Little Glass Slipper*

**GERMAN**
Corrin, Sara & Stephen. *The Pied Piper of Hamelin*
Grimm, Jacob & Wilhelm. *Cinderella*
      *The Fisherman and His Wife*
      *The Frog Prince*
      *Hansel and Gretel*

*Princess and the Frog*
*Snow White*
*Snow White and the Seven Dwarfs*
Lund, Janet, & Laszlo, Gal. *The Twelve Dancing Princesses*
Mayer, Marianna. *The Twelve Dancing Princesses*
Zelinsky, Paul O. *Rumpelstiltskin*

**GREEK**
d'Aulaire, Ingri & Edgar. *Book of Greek Myths*
Hodges, Margaret. *The Arrow and the Lamp: The Story of Psyche*
Hutton, Warwick. *Theseus and the Minotaur*
McDermott, Gerald. *Sunflight*

**ITALIAN**
dePaola, Tomie. *The Clown of God*
     *The Legend of Old Befana*
     *Strega Nona*

**IRISH**
dePaola, Tomie. *Fin M'Coul: The Giant of Knockmany Hill*

**NORWEGIAN**
Cauley, Lorinda B. *The Pancake Boy*
Galdone, Paul. *Billy Goats Gruff*
Hague, Kathleen. *East of the Sun and West of the Moon*
Willard, Nancy. *East of the Sun and West of the Moon*

## Euro-Asian Cultures

**ARABIAN**
Carrick, Carol. *Aladdin and the Wonderful Lamp*
Manson, Christopher. *A Gift for the King*
Mayer, Marianna. *Aladdin and the Enchanted Lamp*
McVitty, Walter. *Ali Baba and the Forty Thieves*

**ARMENIAN**
Hogrogian, Nonny. *One Fine Day*

**JEWISH**
Freedman, Florence. *Brothers: A Hebrew Legend*
McDermott, Beverly Brodsky. *The Golem*

Singer, Isaac Bashevis. *Mazel and Shlimazel or the Milk of the Lioness*
    *When Shlemiel Went to Warsaw and Other Stories*
Zemach, Margot. *It Could Always Be Worse: A Yiddish Folktale*

**RUSSIAN**
Crouch, Marcus. *Ivan: Stories of Old Russia*
Ginsburg, Mirra. *The Lazies: Tales of the Peoples of Russia*
    *One Trick Too Many*
    *Three Rolls and One Doughnut*
Mikolaycak, Charles. *Babushka: An Old Russian Folktale*
Ransome, Arthur. *The Fool of the World and the Flying Ship*
Silverman, Maida. *Anna and the Seven Swans*
Small, Ernest. *Baba Yaga*
Tolstoy, Alexei. *The Great Big Enormous Turnip*
Zemach, Harve. *Salt: A Russian Tale*
Zvorykin, Boris. *The Firebird*

## Asia

**CHINESE**
Carpenter, Frances. *Tales of a Chinese Grandmother*
Demi. *Liang and the Magic Paintbrush*
Hou-tien, Chieng. *Six Chinese Brothers: An Ancient Tale*
LeGalliene, Eva. *Legend of the Milky Way*
Louie, Ai-Ling. *Yeh Shen*
Mahy, Margaret. *The Seven Chinese Brothers*
Mosel, Arlene. *Tikki Tikki Tembo*
Otsuka, Yuzo. *Suho and the White Horse*
Young, Ed. *Lon Po Po: A Red-Riding Hood Story from China*

**INDIAN**
Brown, Marcia. *Once a Mouse*
Demi. *The Hallowed Horse*
DeRoin, Nancy. *Jataka Tales, Fables from the Buddha*
Jaffrey, Madhur. *Seasons of Splendour: Tales, Myths and Legends of India*
Towle, Faith. *The Magic Cooking Pot*

**JAPANESE**
Hodges, Margaret. *The Wave*
Ishii, Momoko. *The Tongue-Cut Sparrow*

Johnston, Tony. *The Badger and the Magic Fan*
McDermott, Gerald. *The Stonecutter*
Morimoto, Junko. *The Inch Boy*
Yagawa, Sumiko. *The Crane Wife*

**KOREAN**
Adams, E. B. *Korean Cinderella*
Carpenter, Frances. *Tales of a Korean Grandmother*
Ginsburg, Mirra. *The Chinese Mirror: A Korean Folktale*

**TIBETAN**
Timpanelli, Gioia. *Tales from the Roof of the World: Folktales of Tibet*

**VIETNAMESE**
Graham, Gail. *The Beggar in the Blanket & Other Vietnamese Tales*
Lee, Jeanne. *Toad Is the Uncle of Heaven*
Vuong, Lynette. *The Brocaded Slipper and Other Vietnamese Tales*

**International**

dePaola, Tomie. *Tomie de Paola's Favorite Nursery Tales*
Hamilton, Virginia. *In the Beginning*
Jagendorf, Moritz. *Ghostly Folktales*
Leach, Maria. *Whistle in the Graveyard. Folktales to Chill Your Bones*
Williams-Ellis, A. *Tales from the Enchanted World*
Yolen, Jane. *Favorite Folktales from Around the World*

# Appendix B

## NATIVE AMERICAN CULTURAL
## AND LANGUAGE RELATED GROUPS

Appendix B offers geographic information about Native American tribes for the reader who wishes to locate stories from a particular area. I believe that the relatedness of the tribes by language affected the quantity of written tales and the similarity of certain legends among tribes.

A generally accepted theory is that the forebearers of Native Americans came across from eastern Siberia to the Western Hemisphere. The different groups were known as language families, and in historic times there have been as many as fifty such language groups. The language groups split into tribes.

Algonquian is the largest language-related group, scattered from the Atlantic coast to the Rockies. Now the term generally refers to a tribe of the northeast Atlantic coastal area.

The Athabascan language group consists of the Plains Indians, who roamed the Midwest and include Blackfoot, Cheyenne, Pawnee, Assiniboin, Omaha, Comanche, Sioux, Cree, Crow, Osage, Omaha, Ponca, Kansa, Dakota, Winnebago, Kiowa, Mandan, and Lakota tribes.

The Iroquois group includes the Eastern Woodland Indians who formed six nations: Oneida, Seneca, Mohawk, Onondaga, Cayuga, Tuscarora.

The nineteen Pueblo tribes of the Southwest include these diverse language groups: Acoma, Cochiti, Hano, Hopi, Isleta, Jemez, Laguna, Nambe, Picuris, San Juan, Sandia, Santa Ana, Santa Clara, San Ildefonso, Siyatki, Taos, Tewa, Zia, and Zuni.

Wabanaki Peoples of the Northeast include MicMac, Maliseet, Missamaquoddy, Abenaki, Penobscot, and Pennacook.

Five tribes in the southeastern United States became known as the civilized tribes in the 1700s because they adopted the white plantation economy. They were the Creek, Cherokee, Choctaw, Chickasaw, and Seminole. In 1830, the southern whites caused their removal. Those who lived through the severe trek west were placed in reservations in Oklahoma.

Listed below are some of the most common tribes who lived in various areas of the United States and Canada, and whose myths and legends are recorded. This list is not all-inclusive but is intended to help the reader locate Native American lore of local origin. Some of the written tales can be found only in anthropological records; some are published in locally available books and pamphlets; and some are available in nationally distributed children's and adult literature. The most common trickster hero of the tribe is named whenever possible. See Chapter 1 for an explanation of the trickster in folktales told for children.

| LOCATION | TRIBE | TRICKSTER |
|---|---|---|
| Alabama | Alabama | |
| | Koasati | |
| Alaska | Aleuts | Raven |
| | Haida | Raven |
| | Innuits | Raven |
| | Kwakiutl | Raven |
| | Tlingit | Raven |
| | Tsimshians | Raven |
| Arizona | Apache | Coyote |
| | Hopi | Coyote |
| | Navajo | Coyote |
| | Papago | Parrot |
| | Zuni | Coyote and Tarantula |
| California | Chumash | Coyote |
| | Poma | Coyote |
| | Shoshoni | Coyote |
| | Shasta | Coyote |
| Carolinas (North and South) | Cherokee | Rabbit, Turtle |

| | | |
|---|---|---|
| Colorado | Cheyenne | Spider |
| Florida | Miccosukee | |
| | Seminole | |
| Georgia | Cherokee | Rabbit |
| | Hichiti | Rabbit |
| Idaho | Nez Perce | Hare |
| Indiana | Delaware (driven from East) | Hare |
| Iowa | Iowa | Hare |
| | Siouan | Rabbit |
| Kansas | Kiowa | |
| Louisiana | Choctaw | Rabbit |
| Maine | Kennebec | |
| | Passamaquoddy | Wolverine (Lox) |
| | Penobscot | |
| Michigan | Pottawatomi | Wisakedjak (Whiskey Jack) |
| | Ottawa | Rabbit |
| | Ojibway (Chippewa) | Manabozho (Hare) |
| Minnesota | Ojibway | Manabozho |
| | Santee | |
| | Sioux | |
| | or Dakota | Great Rabbit |
| Mississippi | Chickasaw | |
| | Choctaw | |
| Montana | Assiniboines | Spider |
| | Blackfoot (Blood, Piegan) | Coyote |
| | Cheyenne | Wihio (person) |
| | Cree | Wisakedjak (Whiskey Jack) |
| | Crow | Coyote |
| | Gros Ventre | Spider |

| | | |
|---|---|---|
| Nebraska | Pawnee | Coyote, Turtle |
| New Mexico | 19 Pueblo tribes | Coyote |
| | Apache | Coyote |
| | Navajo | Coyote |
| New York | Iroquois | |
| |   Cayuga | |
| |   Mohawk | |
| |   Oneida | |
| |   Onondaga | |
| |   Seneca | |
| |   Tuscarora | |
| Oklahoma | Creek | Rabbit |
| | Osage | Coyote |
| | Wichita | |
| Oregon | Kalapuya | Coyote |
| | Klamath | Coyote |
| | Tillamook | |
| Pennsylvania | Seneca | Turtle |
| South Dakota | Sioux | Iktomi (person) |
| | Lakota | Spider |
| Texas | Comache | Fox |
| Utah | Ute | Coyote |
| | Pahute | |
| Washington | Chinook | |
| | Klickitat | Coyote |
| | Yakima | Coyote |
| Wisconsin | Chippewa | Manabozho (Hare) |
| | Menominee | Nanabush (Hare) |
| | Winnebago | Mastshingke (Hare) |
| Wyoming | Arapaho | Spider |
| | Shoshone | Coyote |

*Canada*

| | | |
|---|---|---|
| Northwest Pacific Coast | Kwakiutl | Raven |
| | Tlingit | Raven |
| | Tsimshian | Raven |
| Central Plains | Blackfeet | Na'pi (old man) |
| | Assiniboin | Spider |
| | Cree | Wisakedjak (Whiskey Jack) |
| | Huron | Fox |
| Maritimes | Micmac | Rabbit |
| | Wabanaki | Wolverine (Lox) |

# Appendix C

**IDEA WEBS FOR SHARING FOLK LITERATURE**

Webbing is a flexible instructional strategy used at all grade levels. The webs in Appendix C are intended to provide a framework of ideas for study from which the teacher can select when planning folktale lessons. The webs demonstrate how a series of lessons can be interrelated rather than sequential. Teachers and children can develop their own webs using these models as a catalyst. See *Webbing with Literature: Creating Story Maps with Children's Books* by Karen Bromley (1991) for ways to use webs with individual stories. The graphics in the three webs are reproduced courtesy of Dynamic Graphics, Peoria, Illinois.

**Structure of Tales**

*Nursery Rhymes*

*Cumulative Tales*
- •Old Woman and the Pig
- •Henny Penny
- •Chicken Little
- •Little Red Hen
- •The House that Jack Built
- •One Fine Day
- •The Great Big Enormous Turnip

*Traditional Tales*
- •Three Billy Goats Gruff
- •Little Red Riding Hood
- •Goldilocks & the Three Bears
- •Rumpelstiltskin
- •The Teeny Tiny Woman
- •The Three Wishes

**Read Aloud**

Involve the listeners

*Before* — predicting
*During* —providing word, phrase
- •chanting
- •choral reading
*After* — responsing verbally, creatively

**Creative Response**

Pantomime
Readers' Theater
Creative Drama
Musical Background
Illustration
Creation of Backdrops

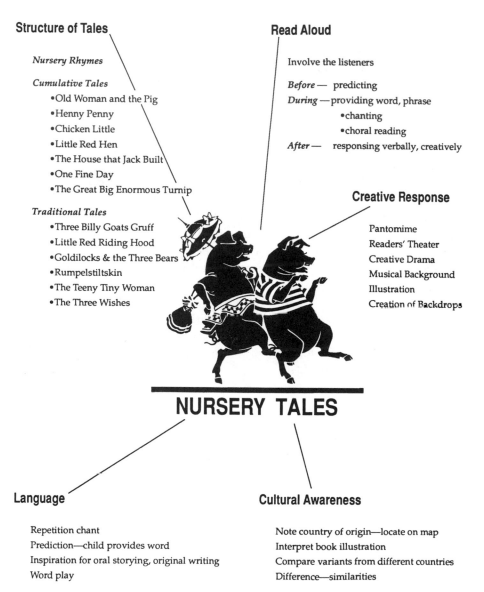

# NURSERY TALES

**Language**

Repetition chant
Prediction—child provides word
Inspiration for oral storying, original writing
Word play

**Cultural Awareness**

Note country of origin—locate on map
Interpret book illustration
Compare variants from different countries
Difference—similarities

**Fairy Tales from Many Lands**

Soviet Union
China
Japan
North America
Norway
France
Germany
Great Britain
India

**Enjoy**

Storytelling
Children as storytellers
Creative play

**Imagine**

Build a magical kingdom
Visualize—build visual
    images
Illustrate

**FAIRY TALES**

**Compare**

*Versions from different countries*
•Cinderella
•Red Riding Hood
•Frog Prince

*Different translations and illustrations*
•Hansel & Gretel
•Sleeping Beauty
•Snow White

*Traditional retold/Modern created*
•Fantasy by
    ∞Jane Yolen
    ∞Oscar Wilde
    ∞Steven Kellogg

**Find the...**

•dream
•wishes
•magic
•task
•motif

**Cultural Legends**

North American Indian
Eskimo
Russian
African
Jewish
Oriental
Greek
Roman

**Critical Reading**

Discover theme:
  •Magic lies in people & creatures
  •Wit & goodness outsmart evil
  •Magical power is limited
  •Universal needs/different responses
Note polarization of characters
Compare/contrast
Transformations

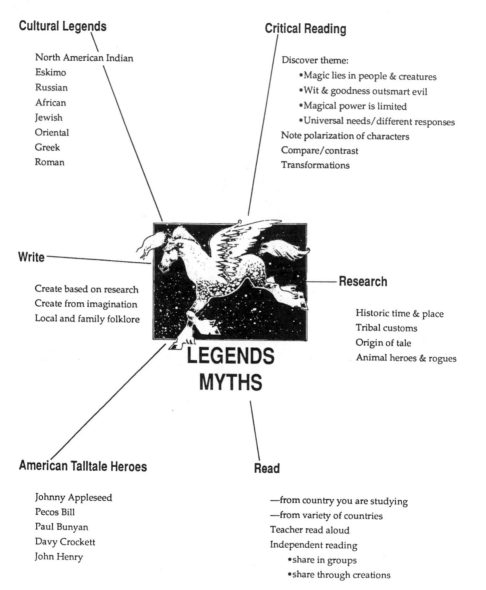

**Write**

Create based on research
Create from imagination
Local and family folklore

## LEGENDS
## MYTHS

**Research**

Historic time & place
Tribal customs
Origin of tale
Animal heroes & rogues

**American Talltale Heroes**

Johnny Appleseed
Pecos Bill
Paul Bunyan
Davy Crockett
John Henry

**Read**

—from country you are studying
—from variety of countries
Teacher read aloud
Independent reading
  •share in groups
  •share through creations

# References

Applebee, A. N. (1978). *The child's concept of story.* Chicago: University of Chicago Press.

Asimov, I. (1961). *Words from the myths.* Boston: Houghton Mifflin.

Banks, J. A. (1987). *Teaching strategies for ethnic studies* (4th ed.). Boston: Allyn & Bacon.

Banks, J. A., & Banks, C. (Eds.). (1989). *Multicultural education: Issues and perspectives.* Boston: Allyn & Bacon.

Bauer, C. F. (1977). *Handbook for storytellers.* Chicago: American Library Association.

Bellville, C. W. (1986). *Theater magic.* Minneapolis, MN: Carolrhoda Books.

Bettelheim, B. (1976). *The uses of enchantment.* New York: Knopf.

Bierhorst, J. (1985). *The mythology of North America.* New York: Morrow.

Bierhorst, J. (1988). *The mythology of South America.* New York: Morrow.

Bierhorst, J. (1990). *The mythology of Mexico and Central America.* New York: Morrow.

Bishop, C. H. (1938). *The five Chinese brothers.* Illustrated by Kurt Wiese. New York: Coward-McCann.

Blatt, G. (Ed). (in press). *Once upon a folktale.* New York: Teachers College Press.

Bosma, B. (1981). *An experimental study to determine the feasibility of using folk literature to teach select critical reading skills to sixth graders.* Ph.D. dissertation, Michigan State University, East Lansing.

Brett, J. (1990). *Beauty and the beast.* New York: Simon & Schuster.

Bromley, K. D. (1991). *Webbing with literature: Creating story maps with children's books.* Needham Heights, MA: Allyn & Bacon.

Bryan, A. (1990, September). *A tender bridge: African-American cultures and storytelling.* Keynote address at the opening session of 22nd Congress of International Board of Books for Young People, Williamsburg, VA.

Calkins, L. (1986). *The art of teaching writing.* Portsmouth, NH: Heinemann.

Chapman, L. (1984). *Discover art* (Vols. 1–6). Worcester, MA: Davis.

Clymer, T., Person, P. D., Johnson, D., Indrisano, R., Venezky, R., Bauman, J., Hiebert, E., & Toth, M. (1989). *A new day.* Needham, MA: Silver Burdett & Ginn.

d'Aulaire, I., & d'Aulaire, E. (1969). *East of the sun and west of the moon.* New York: Viking.

Deitering, C. (1980). *Let's dance.* Searcy, AR: Resource Publications.

Elkind, S. (1975). *Improvisation handbook.* Glenview, IL: Scott Foresman.

Erdoes, R. (Ed.) (1984). *American Indian myths and legends.* New York: Pantheon.

Fijan, C., & Fijan, E. (1973). *Making puppets come alive.* New York: Taplinger.

Fisher, L. (1984). *The Olympians.* New York: Holiday House.

Goss, L., & Goss, C. (1989). *The baby leopard.* New York: Bantam.

Grimm, J., & Grimm, W. (1979). *Hansel and Gretel.* Illustrated by Lizbeth Zwerger. Natick, MA: Picture Book Studio.

Gringhuis, D. (1970). *Lore of the turtle: Indian legends of Mackinac retold.* Mackinac Island, MI: Mackinac Island State Park Commission.

Isaacson, R., & Bogart, G. (Eds.). (1981). *Children's catalog* (14th ed.). New York: Wilson.

Johnson, P. (1964). *Paper sculpture.* Seattle: University of Washington Press.

Kipling, R. (1972). *Just so stories.* Illustrated by Etienne Delessert. New York: Doubleday. (Original work published 1902)

Laliberte, N., & Mogelon, A. (1973). *Masks, face coverings, and headgear.* New York: Van Nostrand Reinhold.

Latshaw, G. (1978). *The theatre student and puppetry: The ultimate disguise.* New York: Richards Rosen Press.

Leach, M., & Freed, J. (1949). *Standard dictionary of folklore, mythology, and legend.* New York: Funk & Wagnalls.

Leese, S. (1980). *Creative dance for schools.* Boston: Plays, Inc.

Lobel, A. (1981). *Fables.* New York: Harper & Row.

*Loon's necklace, The.* (1981). [Film]. Chicago: B. F. Films, Encyclopedia Britannica Educational Corp.

Macaulay, D. (1977). *Castle.* Boston: Houghton Mifflin.

MacDonald, M. R. (1979). *An analysis of children's folktale collections with an accompanying motif index of juvenile folktale collections.* Unpublished Ph.D. dissertation, Indiana University, Bloomington.

MacDonald, M. R. (1982). *The storyteller's sourcebook: A subject, title, and motif index to folklore collections for children.* Detroit, MI: Heal-Schuman.

MacDonald, M. R. (1985). *Twenty tellable tales.* New York: Wilson.

Maher, R. (1969). *The blind boy and the loon and other Eskimo myths.* New York: John Day.

McCaslin, N. (1984). *Creative drama in the classroom* (4th ed.). New York: Longman.

McDermott, G. (Producer), & Wichenhagen, I. (Director). (1975). *The stonecutter.* [Film]. Weston, CT: Weston Woods Studios.

Miller, M. (1988). *In search of spring.* Illustrated by Ian Deuchar. New York: Dial.

Opie, I., & Opie, P. (1974). *The classic fairy tale.* London: Oxford University Press.

Palmer, W. R. (1978). *Why the North Star stands still.* Springdale, UT: Zion Natural History Association.

Paterson, K. (1988). *Park's quest.* New York: Dutton.

Pellowski, A. (1984). *The story vine: A source book of unusual and easy-to-tell stories from around the world.* Illustrated by Lynn Sweat. New York: Macmillan.

Perrault, C. (1985). *Cinderella.* Retold by Amy Ehrlich and illustrated by Susan Jeffers. New York: Dial.

Perrault, C. (1988). *Cinderella.* Translated and illustrated by Diane Goode. New York: Knopf.

Riordan, J. (1984). *Favorite stories of the ballet.* Illustrated by Victor Ambrus. Chicago: Rand McNally.

Rosenblatt, L. (1978). *The reader, the text, and the poem.* Carbondale: Southern Illinois University Press.

Rosenblatt, L. (1983). The reading transaction: What for? In R. Parker & F. Davis (Eds.), *Developing literacy: Young children's use of language* (pp. 118–135). Newark, DE: International Reading Association.

Russell, J. (1975). *Creative movement and dances for children.* Boston: Plays, Inc.

Schonewolf, H. (1968). *Play with light and shadow.* New York: Van Nostrand Reinhold.

Sloyer, S. (1982). *Reader's theatre: Story dramatization in the classroom.* Urbana, IL: National Council of Teachers of English.

Smith, F. (1982). *Writing and the writer.* New York: Holt, Rinehart & Winston.

Smith, F. (1988). *Understanding reading* (4th ed.). Hillsdale, NJ: Erlbaum.

Stauffer, R. G. (1980). *The language-experience approach to the teaching of reading* (2nd ed.). New York: Harper & Row.

Stewig, J. W. (1983). *Informal drama in the elementary language arts program.* New York: Teachers College Press.

Thompson, S. (1955–1958). *Motif-index of folk literature* (Vols. 1–6). Bloomington: Indiana University Press. (Original work published 1932)

Wilde, O. (1968). *The selfish giant.* Illustrated by Gertrude & Walter Reiner. New York: Harvey.

Yolen, J. (1974). *The girl who cried flowers and other tales.* New York: Crowell.

# Index

Aardema, Verna, 5, 20, 28, 46, 57, 67, 86, 89, 95, 111, 112, 146
Aarne, Antti, 8
Acoma legend, 75
Adams, E. B., 20, 113
*Adventures of Nanabush, The,* 121
Aesop, 41, 46, 59, 113
*Aesop's Fables,* 11, 60, 113
Akaba, 58
*Aladdin and the Enchanted Lamp,* 144
*Aladdin and the Wonderful Lamp,* 119
Alexander, Lloyd, 9
*Ali Baba and the Forty Thieves,* 147
*American Tall Tale Animals,* 153
*Anansi and the Moss-covered Rock,* 33, 140
*Anansi the Spider,* 10, 46, 57, 78, 145
*And It Is Still That Way,* 73
Andersen, Hans Christian, 9
Animal Tales
  categories, 10
  definition, 9
  fables, 11
  pourquoi, 12, 79
  trickster, 10
  writing, 78
*Anna and the Seven Swans,* 58, 151
*Anna Banana: 101 Jump-rope Rhymes,* 77, 121
Applebee, A., 5
Appreciating book art, 56, 91. *See also* Illustrations
*Arabian Nights, The,* 119, 144, 147
*Arrow and the Lamp, The,* 136
*Arrow to the Sun,* 47, 57, 146
*Arroz Con Leche,* 20, 57, 123
Asimov, Isaac, 96

*Baba Yaga,* 30, 55, 58, 152
*Babushka,* 58, 125, 147
*Badger and the Magic Fan, The,* 140

Baker, Olaf, 114
Bang, Molly, 4, 67, 114
Banks, James, 23
Baylor, Byrd, 47, 73, 114
*Beauty and the Beast,* 144
*Beggar in the Blanket, The,* 130
Bernstein, Margery, 28, 47, 72, 115
Bettelheim, Bruno, 5
Bierhorst, John, 10, 17, 46, 57, 78, 115
*Billy Goats Gruff,* 127
Blackmore, Vivien, 17, 57, 116
Blume, Judy, 73
*Book of Greeks Myths,* 123
*Bringing the Rain to Kapiti Plain,* 5, 67, 95, 111
*Brocaded Slipper and Other Vietnamese Tales, The,* 19, 156
*Brothers: A Hebrew Legend,* 4, 126
Brown, Carol, 2, 33, 57
Brown, Marcia, 2, 46, 117
Bruchac, Joseph, 18, 49, 118, 126, 133
Bryan, Ashley, 16, 28, 46, 62, 78, 117
*Buffalo Woman,* 47, 129
Bunyan, Paul, 12
Burkert, Nancy, 21, 133

Caduto, Michael, 18, 49, 118, 126, 133
Carew, Jan, 38, 60, 119
Carpenter, Frances, 119
Carrick, Carol, 119
Carrick, Donald, 119
*Castle,* 91
Cauley, Lorinda, 120
Charts,
  comparison, 105
  in pre-writing, 67, 78
  in writing, 79
  of Cinderella tales, 50
  of idioms, 41

Charts, (*cont.*)
  plan for pourquoi tale, 79
  plan for trickster, tale, 78
  story mapping, 31
  story structure, 71
Chase, Richard, 16, 120
Chen, Tony, 112
*Chinese Mirror: A Korean Folktale, The,* 47, 128
Cinderella, 5, 45, 50, 51, 69, 88, 131, 149
Circular map, 36. *See also* Story mapping
Cleaver, Elizabeth, 154
Climo, Shirley, 120
*Clown of God, The,* 85, 124
Coatsworth, Emerson, & Coatsworth, D., 121
Cole, Joanna, 77, 121
Comparisons
  books and films, 53
  Cinderella tales, 51
  legends and myths, 47
  myths with similar themes, 49
  variants of the same tale, 50
*Complete Tales of Uncle Remus, The,* 135
Comprehension
  guiding, 30
  related to critical reading, 43
Conover, Chris, 121
Cooney, Barbara, 57, 116
Corrin, Sara & Corrin, Stephen, 122
*Country Mouse and the City Mouse,* 46
Courlander, Harold, 122
*Cow-tale Switch, The,* 122
*Crane Wife, The,* 157
Critical reading
  analyzing and evaluating conclusions, 55
  as skill, 43
  classifying, 44
  comparing artists' interpretations, 57
  making judgments, 54
  making relevant comparisons, 47
  recognizing theme, 58
*Cross Your Fingers, Spit in Your Hat,* 150
Crouch, Marcus, 23, 122
Cumulative tales, 67, 70
Curtis, Edward, 115

D'Aulaire, Ingri & D'Aulaire, Edgar, 123
Dance, 88
*Dancing Granny, The,* 28, 117

*Dancing Teepees,* 57, 152
*Day It Snowed Tortillas, The,* 135
Delacre, Lulu, 10, 57, 123
Demi, 28, 47, 58, 60, 123
dePaola, Tomie, 17, 28, 31, 57, 67, 84, 124
DeRoin, Nancy, 46, 125
Dewar, Bob, 122
*Diane Goode Book of American Folk Tales & Songs, The,* 130
Dillon, Leo & Dillon, Diane, 57, 86, 116, 112, 119, 134
Directed reading-thinking activity, 35
Dramatizations, 84
*Duffy and the Devil,* 158

*East of the Sun, West of the Moon,* 85, 133, 136, 145, 156
*Egyptian Cinderella, The,* 120
Erdoes, Richard, 10
Esbensen, Barbara, 60, 126

Fables, 46–47, 113–114, 125
  definition, 11
  dramatizing, 85
  understanding themes, 59
  Writing, 80–81
*Fables of LaFontaine, The,* 148
*Fables of Leonardo da Vinci,* 155
Fairy Tales
  as models for writing, 68
  characteristics, 9
  comparing modern and traditional, 81
  comparing variants, 50
  definition, 9
  study of, 91
*Favorite Folktales From Around the World,* 55, 157
Figurative language, 1, 48
  metaphors, 41
  similes, 41
  idioms, 40
*Fin M'Coul: The Giant of Knockmany Hill,* 124
Finger, Charles, 126
*Fire Bringer, The,* 23, 44, 47, 112, 136, 159
*Firebird Suite,* 88
*First Morning: An African Myth,* 28, 72, 115
Fisher, Leonard, 123
*Fisherman and His Wife, The,* 4, 5, 67, 93, 131, 139

*Flapdoodle,* 150
Folk literature. *See also* Folktales
  African American folktales, 16, 163
  Appalachian tales, 16, 163
  by region and culture, 161–167
  classification, 7
  Creole tales, 16, 163
  definition, 8
  importance of, 1
  in multicultural education, 15
  Mexican, 17, 163, 164
  Native American, 18, 162, 170
  translation, 19
Folklore, 23
  classifications, 8
  collecting, 77
  oral, 73
  recording, 83
  regional, 15, 18
  role of masks, 86
Folktales, 3
  adapting, 6
  characteristics, 4
  criteria for evaluation, 7
  definition, 8
  form of, 66
  models for writing, 65
  types, 9
  universality, 3
*Fool of the World and the Flying Ship, The,* 5, 58, 149
Freedman, Florence, 4, 126
*Frog Prince, The,* 131
*Froggie Went A-courting,* 121

Gackenbach, Dick, 127
Gag, Wanda, 127
Galdone, Paul, 5, 27, 66, 67, 127
Gammell, Stephen, 57, 114, 152
*Ghostly Folktales,* 140
*Gift for the King, A,* 144
*Gingerbread Boy, The,* 66, 127
Ginsburg, Mirra, 15, 38, 47, 59, 128
*Girl Who Cried Real Flowers, The,* 81
*Girl Who Married a Ghost, The,* 115
Goble, Paul, 18, 47, 57, 129, 150
*God on Every Mountain Top, A,* 47, 57, 114
*Gold and Silver, Silver, and Gold,* 150
*Golem, The,* 4, 145
Goode, Diane, 51, 130, 152

Graham, Gail, 130
*Grandfather Tales,* 16, 120
*Granny Will Your Dog Bite,* 147
*Great Big Enormous Turnip, The,* 64, 70, 154
Grifalconi, A., 57
Grimm, Jacob & Grimm, Wilhelm, 4, 5, 51, 67, 69, 131, 132, 133
Gringuis, D., 19

Hague, Kathleen, 133, 145
Hague, Michael, 113, 133
Haley, Gail, 49, 57, 133
*Hallowed Horse, The,* 47, 123
Hamilton, Virginia, 4, 16, 24, 47, 123, 133
*Hansel and Gretel,* 21, 132
Harris, Christie, 18, 134, 135
Harris, Joel Chandler, 135
Hayes, Joe, 135
Heins, Paul, 132
*Henny-Penny,* 5, 66, 67, 128
*Her Seven Brothers,* 57, 129
Hertzog, G., 122
Hinajosa, Francisco, 17, 136
Hodges, Margaret, 57, 136
Hogrogian, Nonny, 5, 67, 95, 131, 137
Holder, Heidi, 113
Hooks, William, 16, 137
Hou-tien, Chieng, 58, 138, 146
*How Glooskap Outwits the Ice Giants,* 148
*How Many Spots Does a Leopard Have?,* 46, 55, 142
*How Summer Came to Canada,* 72, 115, 154
*How the Birds Changed Their Feathers,* 155
Huck, Charlotte, 138
Hutton, Warwick, 139
Hyman, Trina, 132, 137

*Itkomi and the Berries,* 129
*Itkomi and the Boulder,* 130
Illustrations
  and cultural understanding, 20
  by children, 34, 60
  compared with film, 54
  criteria, 7
  study of book art, 56, 91
  worthy of note, 111
Improvisations, 84
*In Search for Spring,* 81
*In the Beginning,* 4, 47, 123, 133
*In the Night, Still Dark,* 143

*Inch Boy, The,* 148
Informal writing, 70
Isadora, Rachel, 132
Ishii, Momoko, 139
*It Could Always Be Worse,* 67, 159
*Ivan: Stories of Old Russia,* 23, 122

*Jack Tales, The,* 16, 120
Jaffrey, Madhur, 139
Jagendorf, Moritz, 140
Jarrell, Randall, 93, 131, 133
*Jataka Tales,* 11, 46, 125
Jeffers, Susan, 132
Johnston, Tony, 140
Jotting books, 44, 49
*Just So Stories,* 12

*Keepers of the Earth,* 18, 49, 118, 133, 141
Kimmel, Eric A., 33, 140
Kipling, Rudyard, 12
*Knee-high Man, The,* 16, 142
Kobrin, Janet, 72, 115
*Korean Cinderella,* 20, 113

*Ladder to the Sky,* 60, 126
*Lady of Guadaloupe, The,* 17, 57, 85, 124
Laird, Elizabeth, 140
Language,
    exploring, 94
    expressive, 1
    figurative, 40, 41
    patterns. *See also* Story patterns
    word origins, 95
Laszlo, Gal, 143
*Lazies: Tales of the People of Russia, The,* 38, 59, 128
Leach, Maria, 23, 141
*Leatherman, The,* 127
LeCain, Errol, 122, 149
Lee, Jeanne, 141
*Legend of Old Befana, The,* 125
*Legend of Scarface, The,* 112, 150
*Legend of the Bluebonnet,* 124
Legends
    characteristics, 13
    compared with myths, 47, 48
    comparing similar themes, 59
    definitions, 12
    legendary characters, 12
Lent, Blair, 58, 137

Lester, Julius, 16, 46, 55, 78
*Liang and the Magic Paintbrush,* 28, 58, 124
*Lion and the Ostrich Chicks, The,* 16, 117
Lobel, Arnold, 80
*Lon Po Po,* 158
*Loon's Necklace, The,* 42, 53, 86, 154
*Lore of the Great Turtle, The,* 19
Louie, Ai-Ling, 19, 23, 58, 143, 149
Lund, Janet, 143

Macaulay, David, 91
MacDonald, Margaret Read, 7, 8, 50, 111
*Magic Cooking Pot, The,* 154
Mahy, Margaret, 144
Manson, Christopher, 144
Martinez-Ostos, Susana, 57
Mask making, 86
Mayer, Marianna, 2, 144, 145
Mayer, Mercer, 144
*Mazel and Shlimazel,* 58, 94, 151
McDermott, Beverly, 4, 145
McDermott, Gerald, 28, 46, 47, 57, 78, 144, 145
McVitty, Walter, 147
Mikolaycak, Charles, 58, 125, 147
Miller, Moira, 81
Milnes, Gerald, 16, 147
Monroe, Jean, 147
Moore, Marianne, 148
*More Tales of Uncle Remus,* 142
Morimoto, Junko, 148
Mosel, Arlene, 47, 58, 62, 67, 148
Moser, Barry, 133, 156
*Moss Gown,* 137
Motif index, 81
Motifs, 7, 8, 9, 81
*Mountain Goat of Temlaham, The,* 135, 155
*Mouse Woman and the Mischief Makers,* 134
*Mouse Woman and the Vanished Princess,* 134
*Mufara's Beautiful Daughters,* 221, 57, 153
Multicultural education
    additive approach, 23
    contributions approach, 23
    international study unit, 22, 91
    social action approach, 24
    transformation approach, 24
Music, 87
Myths,
    characteristics, 13
    compared with legends, 47, 48

definition, 12
introducing, 105
writing, 71

*Naked Bear, The,* 46, 116
Norman, Howard, 148

*Old Lady Who Ate People, The,* 136
*Olympians, The,* 123
*Once a Mouse,* 33, 46, 117
*Once More Upon a Totem,* 135
*Once Upon a Totem,* 135
*One Fine Day,* 5, 67, 95, 137
*One Trick Too Many,* 128
Ormerod, Jan, 131
Otsuka, Yuzo, 149
*Ox of the Wonderful Horns, The,* 16, 46, 78, 118
Oxenbury, Helen, 154

Palmer, William, 19
*Pancake Boy, The,* 120
Pantomime, 84
Parker, Robert, 126
Parnall, Peter, 57, 136
Paterson, Katherine, 139
*People Could Fly, The,* 16, 24, 134
Perrault, Charles, 45, 51, 69, 149
*Pied Piper of Hamelin, The,* 122
Pinkney, Jerry, 142
Pourquoi tales, 12, 79.
   *See also* Animal tales
   writing, 79
Pre-writing, 64
   sentence building, 67
*Princess and the Frog, The,* 132
*Princess Furball,* 138
Puppetry, 90

*Rainbow People, The,* 16, 61, 157
Ransome, Arthur, 5, 58, 149
Readers Theater, 30, 88, 91
   conventions of, 89
Reading aloud, 26
   by children, 29
   for language response, 27
   for predictions, 28
*Riddle of the Drum, The,* 57, 112, 146
*Ring in the Prairie, The,* 116

Riordan, James, 88
*Road to Bethlehem, The,* 140
*Rumpelstiltskin,* 21, 158

*Saint George and the Dragon,* 137
*Salt: A Russian Tale,* 159
San Souci, Robert, 16, 150
Sanderson, Ruth, 158
*Scary Stories to Tell in the Dark,* 151
Schwartz, Alvin, 77, 150
*Seasons of Splendour,* 139
*Selfish Giant, The,* 81
*Seven Chinese Brothers, The,* 144
Shulevitz, Uri, 58, 149
Silverman, Maida, 58, 151
*Simple Simon,* 122
Singer, Isaac Bashevis, 94, 151
*Six Chinese Brothers,* 58, 138, 146
*Sleeping Beauty, The,* 88, 158
Small, David, 30, 58, 151
Small, Ernest, 152
Sneve, Virginia Driving Hawk, 57, 152
*Snow White,* 132
*Snow White and the Seven Dwarfs,* 133
*Sorcerer's Apprentice, The,* 88, 127
*Spirit Child,* 17, 19, 57, 116
*Standard Dictionary of Folklore, Mythology, and Legend,* 8, 13
*Star Boy,* 150
*Star Maiden, The,* 126
Steele, Flora, 139, 152
Steptoe, John, 21, 57, 153
Stevens, Janet, 46, 153
*Stone Soup,* 2, 117
*Stonecutter, The,* 146
Story mapping, 30, 70, 105
   chart, 31
   circle story, 33, 36
   flow chart, 34
   for writing, 108
   story staircase, 33, 35
   use in writing, 70
   variants, 33
Story patterns, 2, 5
   cumulative, 5, 27
   repetitive, 5, 27, 64
Story structure, 4.
   *See also,* Story mapping
*Story, A Story, A,* 49, 57, 133
*Storyteller's Sourcebook, The,* 8, 50

Storytelling, 16, 26, 59, 79, 87, 98–99
  by children, 102
  preparation, 107, 118
  tradition, 6, 9
Stoutenberg, Adrien, 153
Stravinsky, Igor, 88
*Strega Nona*, 67, 85, 125
*Suho and the White Horse*, 23, 58, 149
*Summer Maker, an Ojibway Indian Myth, The*, 47
*Sunflight*, 28, 146

*Tales from Silver Lands*, 126
*Tales from the Enchanted World*, 156
*Tales from the Roof of the World*, 54, 61, 153
*Tales of a Chinese grandmother*, 119
*Tales of a Korean grandmother*, 119
*Tales of Trickery from the Land of Spoof*, 151
*Tales of Uncle Remus*, 16, 46, 78, 142
*Talking Eggs, The*, 16, 150
*Tattercoats*, 139, 152
*Telling Fortunes*, 151
Theme,
  in fables, 59
  recognizing same theme in different stories, 58
  unstated, 60
*Theseus and the Minotaur*, 139
*They Dance in the Sky*, 142, 147
*Third Gift, The*, 38, 60, 119
Thompson, Stith, 8
*Three Billy Goats Gruff*, 66
*Three Pigs and the Fox, The*, 138
*Three Rolls and One Doughnut*, 15, 129
*Tiger Eyes*, 73
*Tikki Tikki Tembo*, 47, 58, 62, 67, 118, 148
Timpanelli, Gioia, 54, 61, 1453
*Toad is the Uncle of Heaven*, 141
Tolstoy, Alexei, 64, 70, 154
Tomes, Margot, 127
*Tomie dePaola's Favorite Nursery Tales*, 125
*Tongue-cut Sparrow, The*, 139
Totems, 98
  building, 106
Towle, Faith, 154
*Town Mouse and the Country Mouse, The*, 153
Toye, William, 42, 53, 72, 86, 115, 135, 154
Trickster tales, 10, 17, 78
  list of tricksters, 11
  writing, 78–79

Troughton, Joanna, 155
*Turtle Knows Your Name*, 62, 118
*Twelve Dancing Princesses, The*, 2, 143, 145
*Twister of Twists, A Tangle of Tongues, A*, 151
Type index, 8

Venn diagram, 48
  comparing myths and legends, 47
  of Cinderella versions, 51, 52
  of legends and myths, 48
Vidal Beatriz, 111
*Village of Round and Square Houses, A*, 57, 131
Vinci, Leonardo, 155
Visual art, 91
Visual imagery, 92
Vocabulary,
  development, 37
  figurative language, 40
  oral and written context, 37
Vuong, Lynette, 19, 156

*Wave, The*, 137
*When Shlemiel Went to Warsaw*, 40, 151
*Where the Buffaloes Begin*, 114
*Whistle in the Graveyard*, 23, 141
*Who's in Rabbits's House?*, 86
*Whoppers*, 151
*Why Mosquitos Buzz in People's Ears*, 46, 112
*Why the Corn is Golden*, 57
*Why the North Star Stands Still*, 19
Wilde, Oscar, 81
*Wiley and the Hairy Man*, 5, 67, 114
Willard, Nancy, 85, 156
Williams-Ellis, A., 156
Williamson, Ray, 147
*Witcracks*, 151
Word origins, 95
Words from the myths, 96
Writing, 63, 64, 67
  animal tales, 78
  computer program, 74
  cumulative tales, 67
  fables, 80
  fairy tales, 81–82
  family folktales, 75
  folktales as models, 64, 65
  group story, 64, 67
  improvement, 110

legends, 73
myths, 71
selecting motif, 81
Writing, informal, 70

Yagawa, Sumiko, 157
Yeh Shen, 19, 22, 23, 58, 143, 149
Yep, Laurence, 16, 61, 157

Yolen, Jane, 9, 55, 81, 157
Young, Ed, 22, 58, 143, 158

Zelinsky, Paul, 21, 158
Zemach, Harve, 158, 159
Zemach, Margot, 58, 67, 131, 151, 159
Zvorykin, Boris, 19, 44, 112, 159
Zwerger, Lizbeth, 113, 132

# About the Author

**Bette Bosma** is a professor in the Education Department of Calvin College in Grand Rapids, Michigan. She began her career as a classroom teacher, taught at every level from kindergarten to ninth grade, and was a middle-school reading consultant. She received her B.A. degree from Calvin College and her M.A. and Ph.D. from Michigan State University. Her research in folktales began in 1981, with a dissertation study focusing on critical reading and folk literature, and continues with both library and active classroom research. She conducts workshops for teachers throughout the United States and Canada on getting children and books together. Publications include journal articles and chapters and essays in edited books on folktales and use of informational books in the classroom.